SELLING
YOUR HOME

CRITICAL DECISIONS
THAT **MAKE** OR
BREAK YOUR DEAL

SELLING
YOUR HOME

CRITICAL DECISIONS
THAT **MAKE** OR
BREAK YOUR DEAL

MICHELLE PALYS
REAL ESTATE EXPERT

Niche Pressworks
Indianapolis, IN

SELLING YOUR HOME: Critical Decisions That Make or Break Your Deal
Copyright © 2025 by Michelle Palys

For permission to reprint portions of this content or bulk purchases, contact Michelle@PalysRealty.com.

Author Photograph by: Cole Harper

Published by Niche Pressworks; NichePressworks.com
Indianapolis, IN

ISBN
Hardcover: 978-1-962956-52-9
Paperback: 978-1-962956-51-2
eBook: 978-1-962956-53-6

Library of Congress Cataloging-in-Publication Data on File at lccn.loc.gov

The views expressed herein are solely those of the author and do not necessarily reflect the views of the publisher.

Disclaimer: This book is for informational purposes only and does not constitute legal or financial advice. This book contains the personal experience of the author. While every effort has been made to ensure accuracy, real estate laws and market conditions vary by location and change over time. Readers should consult with a licensed real estate professional, attorney, or financial advisor before making any real estate decisions. The author assumes no responsibility for actions taken based on the contents of this book. It is not the author's intention to solicit the clients or offerings of other Brokers.

ACKNOWLEDGEMENT

To Aunty Toni, who drove me around with her real estate books in the back seat as a kid and who left family vacations early to take care of her clients.

To my kids, Destini and Aaron, who spent their younger years going to showings with me, hanging out in my office, and eating pizza in the conference room after hours (when you should have been in bed) as I wrote up offers for my clients.

To my village of friends and family who helped with our crazy, busy lives in any way you could, thank you.

To all the agents I've worked with along the way, I've learned something from you.

To every client I've ever helped, I thank you. Without you, this book would not be possible.

Thank you to my mastermind friends, who helped me step into my big goals, and my book team, who helped me take on (and complete!) this daunting task.

To all of you who have supported and cheered me on through all chapters of this book and my life, you have made me who I am today. I am grateful for the light and blessings you are in my life.

TABLE OF CONTENTS

32 YEARS OF REAL ESTATE LESSONS

Newly single with two young kids, I desperately needed to sell my house. What I'd thought would be the perfect home had quickly become a nightmare. The previous owners had promised the world, but the inspection process revealed some significant issues. Unfortunately, the contract I'd signed as an unrepresented buyer in a "for sale by owner" transaction made it impossible for me to get out of the deal without losing my entire deposit, so I moved forward with the purchase despite my reservations. A year later, my circumstances changed. I needed out. I needed to sell — and fast!

I hired a top agent in the area who owned a brokerage with a stellar reputation (or so I thought). She advertised heavily and seemed to understand my situation. Once listed, however, my house sat for months with minimal showings. Every week, the agent placed ads for my home in the real estate booklets, but I couldn't help but feel the repeated advertising made it look like no one wanted my house.

She would often come over and commiserate about her own problems. Sometimes, we'd talk about different marketing strategies, and I'd offer her ideas about taking better photos or creating a new description for my house, but she never changed the listing. She just kept doing the same things over and over. She would even say, "You should get your real estate license and come work for me." I was leaving the area and wasn't impressed with how she worked, so it was a no for me. Still, the thought of getting my license lingered. Real estate *was* something I'd thought about pursuing before my life was turned upside down.

The day of the open house, I arrived after it ended, excited to see how things went. When I opened the door, I saw a tilted head reclining on the couch. It was an agent I'd never met before from my Realtor's office... and she was asleep!

The agent apologized for dozing off, but the damage was done. As the listing neared its expiration, I began searching for a new agent. My current agent didn't seem to have the same concerns as I did. She just seemed happy to have the listing. I didn't understand the market back then or what would drive buyers to my home because she'd never explained that to me. I also didn't know how agents used listings as marketing tools for themselves to bring them more clients.

The day my listing was scheduled to expire, I went to her office to be sure my contract was officially canceled. When I told her I was not re-listing with her, things escalated. In front of an office full of her agents, including the one who fell asleep at my open house, she completely lost it. She shook an advertising book in my face, started yelling, and was almost in tears as she told me about how much money she'd spent advertising my property and how I needed to let her be the one to sell it. If I'd had any doubts about switching agents before, I was 100 percent certain now. She'd had months to try to sell my house.

I quickly found a new agent who had the house under contract with a buyer in three weeks. He was fantastic — professional, effective, and supportive. Months later, when I decided to pursue my real estate career, he was my first phone call. He gave me great advice on figuring out how to choose the right brokerage. He's no longer in the business, but he was one of the best agents I've ever worked with and someone who taught me how to treat clients and offer them the best service.

LEARNING THE ROPES OF BEING A REAL ESTATE AGENT

Once licensed, I joined a brokerage and worked from an office cubicle that was right outside the two main conference rooms where all the closings took place — or fell apart. The walls were thin, the lessons were rich, and I quickly learned what mistakes caused deals to crash and burn. Those insights added to my real estate education, which really began 10 years prior with the first of my own eight transactions. I hit the ground running. Working in a busy office with a variety of agents gave me a wealth of experience. I learned how other agents worked, who kept deals together, who had constant issues with clients, whose deals fell apart, who didn't take care of their clients, and who had the best relationships with their clients. This key information is still relevant today, and knowing how other agents work benefits my clients immensely.

Our office had an in-house mortgage lender who became a good friend of mine. She was good at taking care of clients. On slow days, I would hang out in her office, asking questions and learning a ton of valuable information about mortgages. This experience led me to eventually get my own mortgage license. Not only did I learn about mortgages, but I also often visited the title company operating on the floor below our office. There, I learned about researching deeds, titles, and easements.

Back in those days, we were full-time agents, working in the office or out with clients, writing contracts on the hoods of cars, and faxing offers or hand delivering them. There was no virtual anything, just hands-on, real-life experience. Multiple Listing Service (MLS), an online database of properties for sale, had just come online, and the agents in my office learned it together. We had a great reputation and were one of the top offices in our market.

I felt back then and still feel today, that I was in the business of helping people. Technology has created changes and added conveniences, making it a breeze to work with clients at a distance. But it's always about the clients for me. One constant in this business is that rules keep changing. It has become increasingly important for agents to stay up-to-date on rules and compliance so they can write clear clauses that protect clients, explain changes, strategize and negotiate with buyer agents or unrepresented parties, handle inspection issues, keep tough deals together, and get our clients to closing. Communication with clients was a top priority back then and still is today.

In this book, I'll take you behind the scenes of selling a home through a real estate agent's eyes and point out critical decisions sellers need to make along the way, usually at a time when emotions are running high and logic takes a back seat. I'll share practical tips, red flags, and real stories, and you'll gain insight into finding the best agent to price your home well and sell it in the shortest amount of time for the most amount of money. You'll learn what separates great from not-so-great agents and see how the real estate business is hard work centered around our clients. All this information will give you a strong foundation so you can make great decisions when it's time to sell your home in any market.

CHAPTER 1

BEFORE YOU LIST YOUR HOME FOR SALE

Selling a home is deeply personal. There are memories everywhere, and no matter how strong you are, there's always a point in the process when the emotions hit. It gets hard to think clearly about the next right step to take or identify the best option to get the most money for your home in the shortest amount of time. This is why working with a qualified listing agent who is aligned with your goals for selling your house is so important. The listing agent's job is to be the logical side of your brain when emotions start running high.

LOGIC VS. EMOTION: UNDERSTANDING WHAT DRIVES YOUR DECISIONS

Before signing a listing agreement, sellers are in "logic mode." The listing agent talks the seller through all the details that go into listing their home, and the seller asks practical, fact-based questions about pricing, terms, marketing strategy, and offers. This phase of the process is crucial for building a solid foundation of trust and understanding between seller and agent.

Then, once a seller signs the listing agreement, reality sets in. Fears and questions surface, and they start to think, *What if it doesn't sell?* Overwhelm, anxiety, and excitement flood their thoughts. In my experience, sellers can never accurately anticipate how it's going to feel when selling their home, but emotions are normal and hard to control. Even if a seller is no longer living in the home, it still happens.

Because of this, a professional listing agent becomes the logical part of the seller's brain, which is especially important when all hell is breaking loose in the seller's mind. Stress, overwhelm, small kids to clean up after every morning, or a divorce making it tough for a couple to work together — the emotional toll of selling is surprising to most.

As a seller, you don't want to get in the way of getting your home sold. Even after buying and selling twenty-nine of my own properties, working in the real estate industry, and representing thousands of clients, emotions still hit me hard. I know enough that I can force myself into logic mode, but I will admit, it's hard. I know what you're going through.

One of the best ways to minimize those powerful emotions is to work with your agent on all the details

> One of the best ways to minimize those powerful emotions is to work with your agent on all the details that require logical decisions before you list your house.

that require logical decisions before you list your house. This is when you'll set the right listing price for your home so it sells quickly for top dollar, and you won't have to sit in those emotions for too long. This takes the pressure off and allows you to move on to the next chapter of life.

> **CRITICAL DECISION:** You need a strong listing agent who can logically guide you from listing to closing. Emotions often run high once a listing agreement is signed and can tank a deal. Highly reactive sellers can scare off great buyers, so sellers need a strong buffer and a listing agent who can successfully close a deal while navigating everyone's emotions. Remember, your listing agent is your anchor.

My sellers, Mike and Lauren, were going through a messy divorce and needed to sell their home. They wanted top dollar and decided to look at the Zillow® website to determine how they should price their home. Unfortunately, they were almost $100,000 off what their home was worth based on the condition of their home. I gave them a few alternate prices they could sell for depending on the number of renovations and improvements they could make before they sold.

I offered them three plans. Plan A was the top-dollar option, which meant all the work needed to be complete prior to listing. Plan C was selling the house as-is. Plan B was doing some, but not all, of the necessary work. To help Mike and Lauren make the best decision, I also provided a work list, prioritized by highest-value projects. A critical error sellers often make is working low priority projects that won't increase the price they get for their home. It takes a seasoned agent to assess the value each project will have so you're not wasting time and money. Not all projects will have the same return on investment. In these situations, good planning is critical.

Mike and Lauren needed to sell soon because they couldn't make another mortgage payment. There was a lot on the line. Mike worked multiple jobs and Lauren was home with the kids. Despite all the prompting, explanations, and detailed instructions, Lauren became overwhelmed with emotions and couldn't get any tasks completed. They were stuck. I talked them through the seriousness of the situation and made an immediate plan of action. There was *so much* to do. I had to become, in a sense, the general contractor to coordinate all work to be done.

I gave them a simple list of priority tasks with instructions to complete them in order in case we had to pivot and list their house right away. I laid out the timeline for them to move all possessions out so the contractors scheduled to start renovating their home could start on time. All Mike and Lauren needed to do was stick to the plan.

Mike called in a few favors from family and friends. At times, it was messy, but Mike rallied. The house was emptied, and contractors came through like clockwork. It took constant communication and guidance, but we were getting there. We worked with vendors to take payment at closing, and a relative lent some money with the promise to get paid at closing. Agents who have good, honest relationships with vendors can make this magic happen.

The open house was two days away, and I visited Mike and Lauren's house to take photos so the listing could go live in MLS.

The house looked great; even the basement was empty! Suddenly, I noticed a puddle of water around the boiler. The boiler was older but had just been cleaned and inspected. Was there a leak in the foundation we hadn't seen before? This was *bad*.

We got closer and realized the boiler had died. This was just one more — expensive — hurdle. Fortunately, it wasn't the middle of winter, and they were able to shut it down to stop the leak. Mike got estimates. It looked like the lucky buyers were getting a new boiler. Not part of the plan, but because they'd done so much work to fix up their house, they knew they'd come out ahead and could afford the replacement. I was excited about selling the home. I knew we would get a great price, higher than I originally thought, because they *listened*.

The open house brought fifty groups of buyers! It was a beautiful day. All was going well until Lauren told me she was moving back into the house. *No way*, I thought. *Not on my watch*.

We got multiple offers. One was a cash buyer who, after some negotiating, agreed to close in ten days. Perfect! We were back on track. Mike and Lauren would be selling their home, they would have no more mortgage payments to make, and nobody would be moving back in.

Closing day came, and Lauren wasn't there. Fortunately, I had great rapport with her, and we'd recently talked on the phone, so she knew she was going to get money back at closing. Mike was convinced she wouldn't show up, but I wasn't worried. Fifteen minutes later, she arrived, and the closing went through without a hitch.

Making sure all parties involved with the sale have a good relationship with the listing agent, especially in a divorce situation, is critical for success. The best part was that because they listened to my advice, followed the plan, and did all the things they needed to do to improve their home, they got multiple offers to bid up the price, *and* they got the price they'd initially wanted! This is what happens when you work closely with an agent who can help you get top dollar for your home in the least amount of time.

Most people, Mike and Lauren included, don't have any idea how much some agents do to get them to their goals. They'll probably never know. Mike and Lauren were living in so much emotional hell and had such big tasks to conquer they were in survival mode. We did it together. I'm so proud of them to this day. They told me how they thought they were going to lose their house before someone referred them to me and were so thankful for the success we shared in getting their home sold.

Selling a home is emotional — plain and simple. Even when sellers think they're prepared, the process is never as simple as it seems. Don't underestimate how it will affect you. Make sure you hire a professional listing agent with a good reputation who can handle the emotions and keep things on track to get you the best deal for your home in the shortest amount of time. The right agent will make all the difference.

EQUIPPING SELLERS WITH KNOWLEDGE FROM THE START

The best way to avoid potential emotional overload during the selling process is to equip yourself with all the information you need to make logical decisions early on. Here are some of the topics you should cover in your early conversations with your agent:

1. Your goals and timeline
2. Whether you're just selling or buying too
3. Any debt you may have on the home
4. The current condition of your home, necessary repairs or updates, and a completed Property Disclosure form
5. Market analysis and pricing to sell
6. Reasonable changes to customize your listing agreement
7. Photography, marketing, and the home's MLS listing details
8. How to reach buyers
9. Your desired showing instructions
10. Communication and feedback expectations
11. How to accept an offer
12. The process from contract to closing

You can find a full list of questions to discuss with your agent on my website at CriticalDecisionsBooks.com/Resources.

Sometimes, sellers are well-informed and have their finger on the pulse of the real estate market, but they need that trusted partner to manage all the details of the sale to get to a smooth closing. Other times, sellers haven't sold a home in decades, they're selling under strained circumstances, or the details are too much to think about. It's my job as a listing agent to answer sellers' questions, educate them about the process, and set realistic expectations. Most importantly, I clarify lies, myths, and misinformation they might have heard from friends, the news, or found online.

These conversations I have over and over with my clients are at the heart of why I'm writing this book. In all my years in real estate, I often talk with sellers who don't understand the reality of selling a home or, more importantly, everything included in the process. Although my area of expertise is the New Hampshire real estate market, most of the information, advice, and principles I share in this book are relevant regardless of location or market conditions. I hope you find some great information to help you make great decisions when you sell your home.

HOME-SELLING LIES MANY SELLERS BELIEVE

Here's everything you need to know about the five most frequent false beliefs I hear from many of my clients early in the process of selling their homes.

Lie #1: Selling in a Seller's Market Guarantees a High Price

There is a basic expectation among buyers that a home has been kept up-to-date. To sell at fair market value, the home must be of comparable condition to others in that location. If a home has not been repaired or updated, systems haven't been maintained, and they show they need replacement in the next twelve months, that home will be valued lower than those others, regardless of how active the market is or how much prices are increasing on other homes. Outdated homes or homes in need of many repairs will sell for below market value if sold as-is.

Also, starting with a price that is too high will work against you. Your best buyers will never even see it. Most buyers search at their max range of affordability. This is something sellers rarely think about. If your home is worth $765,000 and you list at $810,000, buyers will never search that high and miss your property altogether. They'll only see it when you have a significant price reduction to where you should have priced it originally.

Lie #2: The Zillow Website Provides an Accurate Representation of What My Home Will Sell For

Relying on the Zillow website can be very misleading. The Zillow website uses a computer program that pulls information from MLS, tax data, and the property's listing history and shows you the information in a format that prioritizes photos so you'll spend more time on their site. The Zillow website doesn't know if your home has been updated, needs significant repairs, or has specific issues like a leaky roof. That information can only be gathered in person, as those details come up when an agent is viewing the property to find its top price in the market.

The Zillow website just provides results from an algorithm, not a professional evaluation. The site is designed to get buyers to click on listings and schedule a showing — not with the listing agent, but with a buyer agent who is paying for your information. Basically, part of their business model is to sell buyer info to buyer agents as leads. The Zillow website is an advertising platform designed to make money from agents. However, not all agents get sucked into paying for leads, so looking at the

Zillow website for agents won't show you all the agents in your area. Some of the best agents out there will never be found on the Zillow website.

Sellers naturally want to get the most for their home and I'll admit, the Zillow website is well done with a nice layout and entices most consumers. Even my buyers will send me listings they like that they found on the Zillow website. Unfortunately, their site does no favors for sellers. It also doesn't represent "for sale by owner" properties in a search. The best way to price your home to make the most money on the sale is by working with a knowledgeable, professional listing agent who understands the intricacies of your local market and has access to real market data in MLS.

Lie #3: My Neighbor Sold Their Home for an Incredible Price, So I Should Be Able to Get the Same Amount for Mine

It's easy to get caught up in comparing your property to others in the neighborhood, especially when you see lots of activity around a new listing. But the true story of a home's condition isn't always visible from the outside. A home with lots of showings might still be overpriced if no offers are coming in, and even if offers are being made, they might not match the asking price.

Just like you are different from your neighbor, your home is different too. They might be on a level lot while your driveway is on a hill. They might have water in the basement; yours might be dry. They might have great water pressure, but you need to have your well redrilled. One side of the street might be sunny, but the other is in shade, so the driveway is a sheet of ice all winter. You may not share that information, but a quick check of a phone compass by a savvy buyer will tell them your driveway is on the north side of the road, and that's all they need to know. These types of details all impact what buyers will pay for your home.

Lie #4: It's Best to Wait for the Perfect Offer

The best offers you're going to get are usually the first or second offer. This is because there is a high level of competition when a property is first listed. A buyer knows it's early in the listing and doesn't want the competition to buy it. If your house is priced right and the buyers don't want to lose the deal, especially if it's a home in great condition in a great location, they may offer over the asking price. Sure, sometimes you get lowball offers up front, but those are obvious. If you get one low offer and no other offers within the first three weeks, that just may be the best offer.

If you've had this experience of getting few or low offers, it's likely because your home was incorrectly marketed or overpriced. Occasionally, it's just a buyer "fishing" to scoop a property for less than market value, but that happens less often these days now that all listings are online. In certain times of the year, like around the holidays, it's reasonable to wait three or four weeks after the house has been listed to get a sense of the offers you can expect to receive. Even then, a great property can get an offer in a few days. Days on market is the key.

Lie #5: All Agents Bring the Same Value

As you may have already begun to see, this is 100 percent untrue. I address how to choose a listing agent in Chapter 2, but just know that finding the right listing agent isn't as easy as hiring the first agent you find. Not all agents are created equal.

Something to consider when selling (or buying, for that matter) is that agents who work with both buyers and sellers can provide valuable insight into the pricing strategy and process of selling your home. Whereas agents who work *only* with sellers or *only* with buyers have a limited perspective. Similarly, agents who work part-time instead of full-time have less time to commit to their real estate clients.

In my opinion, the best real estate agents have made a full-time commitment to their clients and career, work with both buyers and sellers, and have personal experience in buying and selling with multiple transactions of their own.

KEYS TO A SUCCESSFUL SALE

1. Selling a home is inherently emotional, and having an agent who can keep you anchored in logic — through accurate pricing, market knowledge, and expert guidance — will minimize stress and prevent deals from falling apart.

2. Overpricing your home based on estimates listed on the Zillow website, neighbors' outcomes, or wishful thinking typically leads to fewer or weaker offers. An accurate market analysis, grounded in current data and your home's true condition, is the best path to securing strong, qualified offers early on.

3. Common misconceptions — such as thinking every seller's market guarantees top dollar or assuming all agents provide the same value — can lead to disappointment and lost opportunities.

CHAPTER 2

CHOOSING YOUR LISTING AGENT

It's time! You've made the decision, and you're ready to sell. But now the anxiety sets in. Will it sell? Who do we call? How much can we get for it? How much will it cost us to sell? Will we have to do repairs? What about that unfinished kitchen project? Will anyone notice the stain on the bathroom ceiling? How quickly can we get through this process? Where do we start?

You know your first move should be to contact a real estate agent, but that thought brings up a whole new set of fears, so you say, "Let's just call our neighbor. I've seen the signs for his business on his car door, so he must be good. He'll do a good job for us because he's right in our neighborhood."

After thinking about it for a few minutes, you change your mind and say, "I suppose we could call Carol. But wait... she's had a sign at our neighbor's house that's been there forever, so maybe she's not that good. I see her company's signs out in front of two other homes around the corner. Is that good or bad that her office has multiple signs in our neighborhood? Is something going on that we missed?"

At this point, your partner chimes in and says, "You know what? We should just call Cousin Judy. She lives an hour away, but she would be mad if we didn't call her first. I wonder if she's back from Florida. I know she travels a lot. She would do a good job, right?"

STOP. STOP. STOP.

It doesn't have to be like this.

When you're thinking about selling your home, the number one way to eliminate the overwhelming anxiety is to find the best real estate agent to work with. This individual should not be the first person you can think of with a real estate license or the agent in your area with the lowest fees. Spend time to find *the one* — the right listing agent who can quell your fears, guide you forward, and help you sell for the highest price possible within your time frame. In this chapter, you'll learn how to assess agents and choose one who's the best fit for your goals.

> When you're thinking about selling your home, the number one way to eliminate the overwhelming anxiety is to find the best real estate agent to work with.

CRITICAL DECISION: The first question most sellers ask an agent is, "What is your fee?" Hiring an agent on fee alone could be the worst mistake you make. Instead, search for a licensed agent in your area who meets your criteria and expectations and is aligned with your goals for selling your home.

WHAT IT TAKES TO BE A REAL ESTATE AGENT

Before I became a licensed real estate agent, I had eight trans-actions buying and selling properties of my own. Each of these deals was an eye-opening experience. Sometimes, an agent did well for me; other times, not so much. Some agents were excel-lent from start to finish, while others made the transaction pain-ful — or didn't even get the job done. Back then, I thought all agents and companies worked the same way. I was wrong. Now, more than twenty years later, I find it's still not easy for people to uncover what's required for a real estate agent to do their job. Fortunately, I'm about to tell you everything you need to know.

Most real estate agents in New Hampshire (and most of the US) are 1099 independent contractors. We get licensed by the state government to sell real estate and choose our own bro-kerage, also called a company, firm, or managing broker. But, as 1099 contractors, we're not employees of the brokerage. The brokerage can't tell us how to do our job as long as we're not violating any rules and regulations.

For example, a brokerage can't require an agent to answer their phone, work a set number of hours per week, sell a certain number of homes per year, or take additional training. There is no regular paycheck. The brokerage pays agents their percentage of the com-mission from each transaction after closing the deal. Some agents have zero or one closing a year; some have fifty or more. Some agents work alone. Some work on a team, and the team (as well as the company) takes a percentage of the commission at closing.

Agents often don't receive 100 percent of the commission paid out at closing, and sometimes it's less than 50 percent.

Most people are surprised when they find this out. New agents often don't realize this either unless they've done their homework. With low home inventory, many agents work part-time or have left the business but still renew their real estate license to keep it active.

To get a real estate license, you must have forty hours of education and pass national and state tests. Then, every two years, agents are required to take twelve hours of training (fifteen hours for Realtors, which is an additional paid designation) to renew their license.

That's it! When people hear this, it blows their mind.

We pass the test, get our license, choose a brokerage company to work under, and can go sell houses. At this point, an agent can legally represent clients in buying or selling one of the most expensive assets they've owned during their lifetime.

The forty hours of training does not include how to write up a Purchase and Sale Agreement (P&S), how to write clauses, how to provide customer service, how to work with clients, or lessons on negotiations and handling objections — none of that. Those skills come from our own life experiences. Some brokerages offer new agent training or mentorship to new agents, but new agents who are really committed to the profession will seek out additional training and mentorship because *they do* want to take great care of clients.

Honestly, it's working with clients where the real training happens.

Once licensed, agents are told to contact everyone they know (in sales, it's known as their *sphere of influence*) to tell them they are now in the real estate business and ask for referrals.

Think about that for a moment. *Forty hours of training, now go sell half-million-dollar homes.*

If you don't do your own research to find the right agent to represent you, you're essentially rolling the dice. Many sellers see a sign in a yard, get a mailer, call their neighbor who sometimes sells houses, hire the first agent they meet at an open house, or work with the first agent they speak with in an office. I'm not saying that's bad — it's how most agents start out — but you *do* need to know how much experience potential agents have. Homes are worth double what they were four years ago, but the training for agents hasn't doubled. And it often shows.

Maybe you meet an agent, they sound nice, they come over to give a listing presentation, and you sign with them. Nice is good, but do you know their level of experience and what they can do for you? You need an agent who understands how to guide you through the process from start to finish. You need an agent who works well with other agents and understands how potential buyers think about buying your home. You need marketing, strategy, and a negotiator. You want an agent who answers their phone and is available. *This is a critical decision that can make or break your deal.*

You need an agent who works well with other agents and understands how potential buyers think about buying your home. You need marketing, strategy, and a negotiator. You want an agent who answers their phone and is available. *This is a critical decision that can make or break your deal.*

HOW AGENTS REPRESENT CLIENTS

A listing agent represents you as a seller, and they'll help you sell your home. If that same agent is also helping you buy a home, that agent will represent you as a buyer agent.

The buyer of your home may have their own buyer agent or a buyer facilitator (the two have different responsibilities, but for this book, I'm going to use the term *buyer agent* to keep it simple), or they may be unrepresented by an agent and call the listing agent directly to see, and perhaps make an offer on, the home. At this point, the seller works for you unless they already had a buyer agency agreement with the buyer, which would create a 'dual agency' situation. Your agent can explain this further.

As a seller, you will pay your listing agent's office a commission, which the office splits with the agent. From the result of a class action lawsuit settled in July 2024, you, as the seller, can also offer to pay the buyer agent's office, who will split the fee with the buyer agent. Ask your agent if this is something you should consider, and they should easily be able to explain the pros and cons. Whatever you decide will then be included in the listing agreement for your house. Any agent should be able to easily explain it, as it is part of the listing agreement.

It's crucial that you know how your agent is representing you. Your agent may be part of a team, a designated agency office, or have other agents helping them who might not be able to represent you as a seller. Sometimes those agents helping your listing agent can only represent buyers. You need to know this upfront and should ask if it's not mentioned to you to protect the integrity of your position as a seller if an offer is made.

A listing agent's fiduciary duty is to the seller. This means that if a buyer comes directly to your listing agent to buy your home and doesn't have an agent, that person is an unrepresented buyer. Your listing agent can help facilitate the paperwork but cannot negotiate on the buyer's behalf. A listing agent negotiates *only* on the seller's behalf, except in rare dual-agency circumstances.

A listing agent's job is to protect the seller's financial interests. If a buyer were to ask me, "What's the lowest price the seller would accept?" I am not at liberty to disclose that information. I could ask the seller if they want me to disclose that, but I am better off writing up the offer with what the buyers want to pay and then speaking with my seller to negotiate my seller's best interests. Getting my seller's house sold is my primary responsibility, according to the listing agreement I have signed with my seller.

I know trying to understand the difference between listing agents, buyer agents, and dual agents is a bit confusing, so ask your agent to explain it in person. If your agent can't explain the differences, that's a red flag. I point it out here so you know there is more to it than meets the eye. Asking about it will open a conversation with your agent, and you will know what to expect.

CRITICAL DECISION: Knowing how your agent works to represent you is important. If you don't, it can jeopardize negotiations. Choose well. Good representation is not cheap. Cheap or inexperienced agents may not represent you well.

FINDING THE RIGHT AGENT FOR YOU AND YOUR HOME

Unless you already have an agent who you know is an absolute gem — someone who works hard, is an expert professional, and will do everything possible to sell your property for the highest price in the shortest amount of time — it's worth exploring your options.

Agent availability is key. You need someone who understands exceptional customer service and can deliver when it matters most. Even if an agent has done well for you in the past, they may not be able to do a good job for you now. Find out before signing with them. Maybe they're heading out of the area for a few months, caring for a sick relative in another state, or dealing with an illness of their own. If that's the case, it's okay to graciously bow out and find someone who can meet your current needs. Another option is to ask them to refer you to another great agent. Don't feel bad. This is your money and your asset at stake. You can remain in contact with them and maybe work with them again down the road. Any good agent will understand and not take it personally. The point is that you absolutely need to find out how available an agent is before you hire them.

Remember, not all agents are created equal. You may have learned this the hard way during a previous sale or heard other sellers' horror stories. And, as I mentioned earlier, even if an agent is licensed, they might only sell one or two properties a year. So, even if the agent you're considering is a dear friend, sibling, or family member, research them and their work a bit before signing a listing agreement with them.

As you begin calling listing agents to find the right fit for you, you'll need to weed out agents who are not able to give you 100 percent. Selling your home is a big financial decision, and whether your house is worth $500,000 or five million, this is your property, your money, and your pocket. You need to protect yourself and your asset by doing some work to find the right agent who will do their best for you. Agents hate to lose listings, so be prepared; some agents don't lose well if you don't sign with them and will say things that might shock you or try to pressure you to sign a listing agreement even if it's not the right fit.

There are some agents who don't like listings that much but like working with buyers. They'll get a listing, put up a sign, take calls from potential buyers, but won't work as hard to sell the listing. Your yard sign is generating business for them, but they're not getting your house sold. When you see signs in a front yard for a long time, think about that. The sign is there for a long time because the listing is not selling. You want that "for sale" sign to go into the ground quick and come out after it sells quickly. You don't want to be a billboard for an agent to grow their business if they're not doing the right things to get your home sold. That said, if your home was marketed well but knowingly overpriced at your request as a seller, that could be why it's sitting longer on the market — that's your fault, not the agent's.

The truth of the matter is that agents want listings. Period.

If you find yourself being pressured by an agent who you know is not going to be available and feel yourself caving in to sign the listing agreement, give yourself and the agent twenty-four hours before doing anything.

If you're strong-willed, self-employed, or highly successful, you might feel the need to take over your agent's job with your ideas and try to control the process. This isn't good for you or the sale. That's why it's so important to pick the right agent from the start. Don't pick an agent you feel you can have control over because you won't be happy, and it will cause issues for both of you.

Interview several agents if necessary, and take the time to find someone who meets your expectations. If you're looking for a referral, I can always help you with that. I have many agent connections throughout New Hampshire and across the country and can find you a great agent. I know the questions to ask them and can evaluate their experience, availability, and marketing to determine whether they're a good fit for you to interview. I can also help if you need a referral to buy a home in a different location and are looking for a buyer's agent.

I WANT TO SELL, BUT I'M NOT READY TO MOVE YET

"But Michelle," you say. "I don't want to sell my home in the shortest amount of time because I don't want to move right away."

Discussing your timeline is an important conversation to have with your listing agent *before* you put your house on the market. Think about it. What if you get an offer on the first day? What would you do? Say no? That would be kind of crazy if it's a good offer, right? You don't want to be in that position because then you might end up sitting on the market for three months, rejecting offers (remember Lie #4 some sellers believe about waiting for the perfect offer that I told you about in the last chapter?).

At that point, buyers will see your home sitting on the market and think, *What's wrong with that house? Why isn't it selling? It must not be worth the listed price.* Buyers will then make a lower offer or pass on your listing altogether. The pool of original potential buyers will be gone as they will buy other houses. To avoid finding yourself in this situation, you want a strategy that gets you to your financial goals and fits your timeline for moving out of the home.

Once you list your house, your goal should be to close a deal in the shortest amount of time, but if you're not ready to move, there are other options for letting people know your house is for sale without officially starting the ticking clock in MLS for the world to see. An off-market listing is one short-term solution.

Some agents are so eager to get a listing that they'll convince you it's a good time to list, even when it's not in your best interest. That's why I'm writing this book. I find sellers in this predicament too often, and they don't know what to do. They've already signed a listing agreement and now feel trapped. That's never a good situation, and it is something that frustrates me about this industry I've worked in for more than twenty years.

If you're not ready to list your house on the market but want to get plans in place to sell soon, find an agent who is willing to have that conversation and be part of the plan. Then, you can sign a listing agreement and delay the active listing date or delay showings. In the meantime, you can work with your listing agent and use their expertise to get ready to sell at the best possible price. This is how it worked with Mike and Lauren. We had to change the active listing date a couple of times when projects weren't fully completed, but it allowed me to dedicate many hours to them with a firm commitment of a listing agreement.

This situation is a win-win for both the sellers and the listing agent. I would not spend a month getting clients ready to sell without it being part of the long-term listing plan. No agent has that kind of time to take away from other clients — especially since you now know agents only get paid after closing. All the hours we work, upfront, dedicated to selling your home, go unpaid until closing. It is the only industry that works that way (that I know of). So, have a conversation with your listing agent about your timeline for moving out of your home early in the process. You'll be surprised at how well things will go for you.

> **CRITICAL DECISION:** Taking expert guidance from your listing agent on a workable timeline will be the easiest way to get the most from your home. Have that conversation months ahead of listing your house, if time allows. You'll be amazed at how well it will all come together with good planning.

I know it's hard to think about picking up the phone and talking with a couple of agents because it can feel like they all want to talk you into an instant appointment or signing a contract right away. *But you must do it.* It will be worth it. And you'll be surprised at the differences you find between agents. Find *the one* who will help you meet your goals.

KEYS TO A SUCCESSFUL SALE

1. Don't just call your neighbor who's an agent or sister-in-law who sometimes sells houses because it seems convenient. Interview multiple agents, ask them detailed questions, and make sure they have a strong plan for pricing, marketing, and working with your specific timeline.

2. A listing agent's primary duty is to the seller, whereas a buyer's agent works for the buyer's interests. Know who's representing whom so you're not caught off guard if your listing agent brings in another agent to host open houses or show your property. Know the agent's role and whether they are representing your property or not.

3. If you need time before moving, discuss off-market or delayed-listing strategies with your agent rather than immediately putting your house on the market. Having this conversation with your agent months before you're ready to sell will make the process go a lot smoother, and you'll have a professional to help you coordinate the important details.

CHAPTER 3

RED FLAGS TO LOOK FOR BEFORE SIGNING A LISTING AGREEMENT

Many seller complaints like, "My agent did a crappy job," "I never heard from my agent," or "My agent left my listing up with 10 bad photos" stem from not asking important questions before hiring an agent and signing the listing agreement. There may have been red flags, but you didn't know what to look for, and the agent sounded very convincing or maybe even discounted your fee when asked (remember what I said in the last chapter: agents want listings).

Your agent should be professional, communicative, knowledgeable about your local market, and proactive in servicing your listing. Don't settle for anything less — this is your home, your asset, and your investment. The best way to identify red flags is during the interview process when you're meeting with potential agents to find one who is the best fit for you.

This chapter is all about helping you identify potential red flags so you can interview agents and ask questions to find a qualified professional who will help you reach your goal. For an additional list of questions and typical responses you'll get from agents, visit CriticalDecisionsBooks.com/Resources.

Now that you know the importance of choosing the right agent for you and your home, here are some common red flags I tell people to look out for when they're interviewing potential listing agents.

- Red Flag #1: Lack of Responsiveness
- Red Flag #2: Limited Availability
- Red Flag #3: Agents Who Aren't Local to Your Area
- Red Flag #4: Not Understanding Buyer Expectations
- Red Flag #5: Overly Restrictive Showing Policies, Agent Ego, and Too Much Control Over the Listing

Some of these things are pretty easy to evaluate. Call the agent a time or two and see if they answer their phone. Send a text or email inquiring about one of their listings or about viewing a listing as a buyer. If they're busy or in an appointment, they might not pick up, but they should still respond quickly. At the very least, you should receive a text.

RED FLAG #1: LACK OF RESPONSIVENESS

In this day and age, it's not hard to reply promptly. A good agent will get back to you within twelve hours — twenty-four hours, max. If they don't, I'd cross their name off your list, even if they're someone you've worked with in the past or someone highly recommended to you. Lives change, and an agent who was great three years ago might be watching their grandkids during the week now and not be spending as much time in real estate.

> **CRITICAL DECISION:** How quickly an agent responds to your initial call or message reflects their patterns and habits. It won't change, even if you ask them to, because habits are ingrained. *How quickly an agent responds to you is a strong indicator of how quickly they'll respond to a buyer interested in your property.* And that responsiveness is *key* to getting your home sold.

Let's say you live near a lake, and you're trying to sell your home. It's a busy weekend in the area, but it's a little dreary, so it's not a great boating or beach day. Visitors who hope to move to the lake are driving around and see a "for sale" sign in front of your property, so they call the number on the sign.

Do you know if your agent will answer their phone? This could be a detrimental moment for you if they don't. You need to know what your agent will do in a case like this. Ask them before hiring them.

If your listing agent is highly responsive, they'll answer or call the potential buyer back right away. If not, that potential buyer could drive off and not return for weeks — or maybe never. If your listing agent doesn't capture buyers when they're actively looking at properties, they're not doing a good job for you.

It always amazes and frustrates me when buyers call me and say, "You answered your phone! You're the sixth agent I called today and the only one who answered."

This happens *all* the time. It's not new, either. In all my years in real estate, I've seen it repeatedly, but now it's worse than ever even though we all have phones on us 24/7.

"I don't like to answer my phone," an agent said to me one day. "I let it go to voicemail and then decide if I want to call them back."

What? Excuse me? I thought. *Phones are our entire business! We take care of people. How can we help people if we don't answer when they need us?*

I believe a lack of responsiveness is the number one problem among real estate agents. If you hire an agent who is non-responsive, you will be 100 percent disappointed at various points along the way. Even if the agent is your best friend, the agent you choose to list with needs to be 100 percent on their game. If they are not, don't hire them to sell your most valuable asset.

RED FLAG #2: LIMITED AVAILABILITY

Many agents did quite well during the booming pandemic housing market because making a sale was quick and easy. An open house would bring multiple offers, and they'd be under contract without inspections with minimal effort. Many of those agents are no longer thriving. Real estate is *not* an easy business. There are many details to follow through on to keep deals together.

You need an agent who is all-in, willing to do all the things needed to close a deal successfully *and* have the hard, strategic conversations with you and buyer agents. You need an agent who will do double duty — for you and the buyer — in case the buyer agent isn't doing a great job for their client (another unfortunate reality that is more common than you know). You want the listing agent who will work hard for you, price your home correctly, help you prepare for sale, and do everything possible to get top dollar for you in the shortest amount of time, leading to a smooth closing.

When I was first getting into real estate with two little kids, I told my manager I wanted to work in real estate part-time. He chuckled and said, "Real estate is not a part-time business. Buyers and sellers work on their schedule, not yours." Right then, I became a full-time agent. Sure, some agents need to work two jobs, but if your agent is working another job and selling houses on the side, it's going to be really hard to get a good outcome. Showings will be a challenge, and communication with you and potential buyers will fall through the cracks.

Your agent's availability will impact how quickly you sell your house. If your dream buyer calls your agent but your agent can't answer or doesn't call back promptly, it's a lost buyer opportunity. And unfortunately, buyers don't always come back. It's also bad for buyer agents who have eager buyers who want to see your home. In this situation, buyers will often say, "I guess they don't want to sell their house," but it's likely not the seller's fault. The worst part is the seller doesn't even know this is happening.

A big challenge is when your listing agent lives too far away and it's not convenient to show your property. Your agent may answer a buyer's call but say, "Hi, I'm showing other properties all day, and it will take me ninety minutes to get there. I don't think today is going to work. Is there another day I can show you the house?"

The buyer responds, "No, we're only in town today. Can we see it later today? We leave tonight."

Your agent apologizes, explains they can't make it work, and says goodbye to a possible ready, willing, and able buyer — maybe one who is looking to buy and close quickly. Some buyers look at many properties in one single day and then make an offer on their favorite one.

It's hard to quantify lost opportunity, but this type of scenario happens more than you realize. The real question is: who really loses here? Sure, your agent misses out on a commission. But that's not the main loss. You, the seller, are the one who loses the most. You miss out on a serious buyer because your agent wasn't available.

Now, what if an agent is local but busy all day? They can't be in two places at once. This is a fair point. Remember, agents are independent contractors and there's no way to mandate availability unless you have this spelled out in your listing agreement (more on listing agreements in Chapter 5). When I'm booked with clients and can't personally be there to show a property, I have a backup plan. Or I may try to sneak the buyers in between other appointments. I also make sure my sellers have flexible showing availability so buyer agents can do single-broker showings. A quick showing is better than no showing, and if the buyers really like the house, we can make another appointment. I won't let a buyer slip through the cracks. Unfortunately, not every agent operates this way. Some do, but not all. You need to know how your agent works at times like these.

When I take a listing, I make it as easy as possible for buyers and buyer agents. I also offer to help buyer agents by showing the home to their buyers even when they are unavailable. We get more done this way. I work for my seller, which means getting every potential buyer in the door is my responsibility. Unfortunately, I run into many agents who will not help in a situation like this.

I know I'm uncovering a bit of the dark side of how some agents work, but it's why I'm writing this book. It's not your imagination when you have a bad experience with an agent. And you don't have to settle for it. This kind of behavior is what gives our industry a bad reputation. Some agents just aren't as available as others. Signs in a yard mean a property hasn't sold yet. Remember that. Some agents are very efficient, and their listings only last a short time on the market before they take their sign down. A sign in a front yard for an extended period isn't a good indicator of the agent's effectiveness (unless it's a new development and there are multiple homes to sell).

While I can't control how others run their businesses, I *can* control how I run mine and how I take care of my clients. I'm not alone — there are many skilled, professional, expert real estate agents in every market. It's just a matter of finding the right one. Most of the agents you speak with will tell you that they are responsive and available. But what does "responsive and available" mean to them? Ask them to explain their criteria to reveal the whole picture of how they work.

This is where you need to play the role of detective. Think of it as solving a little mystery. Dig deeper with questions. Ask yourself: *Who is the best person to sell my home in the shortest amount of time for the most mon-*

> Ask yourself: *Who is the best person to sell my home in the shortest amount of time for the most money?*

ey? If you do your homework upfront, you will feel confident in your decision once you sign that listing agreement.

CRITICAL DECISION: Choosing the right listing agent is the single most important decision you need to make at the beginning of the home-selling process. When you find the right agent, everything else will go much more smoothly. If you do not work hard to find the right agent, you will feel like you're on a bad roller coaster ride and have more anxiety and frustration than you ever imagined.

RED FLAG #3: AGENTS WHO AREN'T LOCAL TO YOUR AREA

You may know and love an agent who does not live near the property you want to sell. Unfortunately, this is a problem because agents living outside an area often struggle to price a home for the local market — something I've seen many times by looking at overpriced listings in MLS. It takes a significant amount of time and experience to comb through local market data in MLS to price the home just right. The market has a pulse, and I believe it's the listing agent's job to stay connected to it.

For example, my expertise is around Lake Winnipesaukee, down through southern New Hampshire and the Bedford area, where I lived and began my career. If you've ever driven through New Hampshire, you'll know it can be time-consuming to get anywhere because of all the mountains, lakes, and our highway system. Even though I had property in the mountains for years, I refer potential clients to agents who live up there, just as I will for buyers and sellers in other parts of the state where I don't work. It's not fair to my seller if I'm not able to service their listing efficiently.

> The market has a pulse, and I believe it's the listing agent's job to stay connected to it.

Just because I *can* list a home anywhere in New Hampshire doesn't mean I *should*. I need to be honest with my seller and tell them this. It is more beneficial to them that I refer out-of-area clients to agents I know who will do an exceptional job for them. Most agents don't want to lose a listing, so they'll take one far away and then price it incorrectly because they don't know the local market. Then, the listing agent might consistently rely on other agents to service their listing because they can't get there, meaning your agent is really not representing you after all. This situation creates stress for both the seller and the listing agent, and I don't think it's fair for the seller, especially if they weren't told how detrimental a non-local agent could be to getting their home sold before they signed the listing agreement.

If your listing agent has a three-hour round trip to show your home, they won't be as available to manage your listing long-term. Sure, in the beginning, they might be enthusiastic, but after two or three weeks — especially if they are busy elsewhere — your home will most often be last on their list. Showings will be limited to their schedule, which could make it impossible for some buyers to ever see your home, especially in bad weather. They also may underprice or overprice by not knowing your home's local market nearly as well as an agent who works in the area. Some agents hate to refer to other agents, even though it would be in the client's best interest. Is that what you want? You need to make that decision with your eyes wide open.

Recently, I helped a buyer put a great home under contract. It was a fantastic property, but the listing price struck me as odd because it was clearly too low for the area and the condition of the home. Before I even looked at the listing agent's name, I knew it was an out-of-area agent simply based on the price they'd listed the home for. These sellers lost at least $40,000. I cover more details about nailing your listing price in Chapter 4, but hiring an agent who knows the market, can accurately price your home, and is available to service your listing makes all the difference when negotiating a successful sale.

When I get calls to take listings outside my area from clients, friends, or family, I carefully evaluate whether I can truly service the listing properly. I look at my calendar, my availability, and my ability to commit to the time and attention the property deserves. If I know I can deliver a five-star experience, I'll take the listing. If I can't, I'll refer it to another agent — someone I know will provide A+ service for my sellers.

Over the years, I've developed a network of agents I trust, and I'm always happy to find and refer to great agents around the country. From California to Texas, Colorado to northern New Hampshire, or even Florida, I can point people to excellent agents in their area simply by asking the right questions. Finding a local agent is a critical decision when selling your home. Don't hesitate to ask potential listing agents where they're based when you're making a hiring decision before you sign a listing agreement contract. An agents office address might be different than the area they live and work in.

RED FLAG #4: NOT UNDERSTANDING BUYER EXPECTATIONS

Not all agents work with buyers. Some work only with sellers. Understanding how buyers feel about various aspects of a property, market prices, and the latest renovation styles are important things to know when it comes to pricing homes to sell. For example, if I'm working with buyers and they say they're seeing homes in the same price range in better or worse condition, have more amenities, or need updates, that's *gold* for my seller. As a listing agent, when I can gather relevant details about the market from a buyer's perspective, my seller benefits.

Working with buyers *and* sellers also helps to recognize early signs of market transitions. When buyers aren't making offers, agents who work with buyers and sellers can look at the overall market and see patterns. But if an agent never works with buyers, they might think there's a problem with the listing and reduce a price prematurely. Understanding buyer expectations and knowing the competition is important. What's selling fast? Where are buyers spending their money? There is valuable information in working with a variety of clients. Experience and information are the gold that an agent who works with both buyers and sellers can provide.

An agent may say, "Well, I work with buyers when they call on my listings, so of course I work with buyers." This is different from working as a buyer agent *and* a listing agent. I'm talking about agents who also work with buyers to look at other properties. Some agents can't be bothered with working with buyers of other listings because it's more time-consuming, and there is quite a variety of homes and buyers. This might not be a problem for you; just know who you're working with. You don't want an agent with a limited perspective on the overall market.

RED FLAG #5: OVERLY RESTRICTIVE SHOWING POLICIES, AGENT EGO, AND TOO MUCH CONTROL OVER THE LISTING

Finally, you don't want a listing agent who has super-restrictive policies for showing your home. It's not about them; it's about getting your home sold. You want buyer agents to bring buyers in, and if your agent is unavailable yet insists on assisted showings, you will have fewer buyers seeing your home. Similarly, an agent who requires a 24-hour notice to show your home is going to miss a lot of opportunities to let buyers visit the property. Many buyers are out driving around when they see a house for sale, and they're not coming back to the area tomorrow. Properties that have overly restrictive showing times and rules get shown less, sit on the market longer, and, sadly, have more price reductions.

I was recently out on a Sunday previewing properties for a new client when I thought of a house I'd seen recently that had been on the market for a while with a few price reductions. I hoped to get in to view the house that day, as I knew it was vacant. The house was not listed in Showing Time, an app agents use to schedule showings of properties, so I called the listing agent and was shocked when she said, "Oh, I don't have a lockbox on the property, and I'm out of town today; could you make an appointment for Tuesday?"

I was shocked. Here was a vacant property with multiple price reductions, and yet it wasn't easy for a buyer agent to show it to an interested buyer. My client said, "Forget it," and never viewed the property.

In another instance, it was freezing out with bitter-cold wind, but I had buyers who were ready to buy and wanted to see a specific property. I called the listing agent, who said, "Well, I don't want to drive all the way over there if you're not sure your buyers have interest in the house."

"I can't guarantee they're going to make an offer if that's what you're asking. They're looking at several homes, but they do need to see inside this one to know if they're really interested," I said.

"Can they make an appointment for tomorrow?" asked the agent.

"No, they're trying to make a decision today. They're cash buyers. Can I show them the house quickly? It might be *the one*," I said.

The agent never let us in. Since then, the home has continued to sit on the market with two price reductions. I'm sure the agent's availability and attitude is one of the reasons why. I always feel bad for the seller in these instances. As agents, it's our job to let sellers know how badly these types of situations work against them. Unfortunately, as licensed agents, we can't contact sellers who are under contract with another agent to offer advice or solutions. It goes against our code of ethics. It is frustrating because we know the sellers have no idea it's happening.

CRITICAL DECISION: If you choose an agent who only does assisted showings or is a strict gatekeeper of your property, realize it might keep out an interested buyer, and they may never see your home. As a seller, you need to understand how important it is to allow showings as often as possible. Allowing buyer agents to bring in interested buyers without your listing agent present (this is called a single-broker showing) is a great way to get more showings. Allowing a lockbox for easy access is another way. Don't let your agent's ego dictate how you allow buyers to see your property. Now that you know it can be severely restrictive talk to your listing agent.

Here's one more example. One Friday afternoon, I was out with buyers, and they were talking about a seven-figure home that just had a price reduction. I called the listing agent, hoping to get my clients in to view the home that night.

I called, then texted.

No response.

We finished looking at homes for the night, and by the next day, I'd still received no response from the listing agent. Fortunately, there was an open house scheduled for that Sunday, and I encouraged my buyers to go. I got there ahead of them and saw the listing agent standing in the kitchen.

"I called and texted you Friday," I said.

"I saw you called," he replied.

That's it. Nothing more.

"Did you get my text saying I had buyers who wanted to see the property?" I asked.

"Yes," he said. "I don't use texting for real estate. Too much can go wrong."

I was floored.

I don't understand how agents can ignore interest in the homes they are supposed to be selling. The seller was a friend of his, but I'm sure the seller had no idea his agent didn't respond to an interested buyer during a busy summer weekend right after a price reduction. My buyers passed. The home eventually sold after four months and a third price reduction.

If you are a seller, make sure you tell your listing agent to find a way to get *any* buyer with interest in to see your home. Buyers often surprise us and make offers on homes out of the blue. Your listing agent is working for you to get your home sold, and they shouldn't deter a showing of your home in any way. Allowing them to turn interested buyers away — for any reason — is bad for your home sale. You'll sit on the market longer and end up taking a reduced price.

KEYS TO A SUCCESSFUL SALE

1. Prioritize responsiveness, availability, and local knowledge when looking for a listing agent. If your agent doesn't answer quickly, works part-time, or isn't familiar with your local market, you risk missed opportunities, incorrect pricing, and a drawn-out market time. For an additional list of questions and typical responses you'll get from agents, visit CriticalDecisionsBooks.com/Resources.

2. Evaluate an agent's location and past listings to see if the agent provides high-quality photos, strong descriptions, and clear marketing. Ask them if they are taking any vacations soon or extended time away. If you don't ask, they may not tell you until it's too late — *after* you sign the listing agreement. Avoid agents who dismiss your concerns.

3. Don't let a listing agent deny buyers access to your home or impose unnecessary constraints. Insist on clear communication, be sure you have professional boundaries in place if you know the agent personally, and don't trust blindly. Ask the important questions and create a plan that aligns with your goals.

CHAPTER 4

LISTING PRICE DOS AND DON'TS

Here's something most sellers don't know: the buyer ultimately sets the sale price for your home.

How, you say?

By what the buyer is willing to pay for it.

Buyers are active in the market and know what's out there as competition because they've been searching for homes similar to yours. They can tell you specific details about the homes listed in their price range, including how the agent presents the property and whether the home is priced right. They've attended open houses; they've looked at and smelled many interiors. Buyers shop online constantly. They look on Zillow.com, Realtor.com, Redfin.com, and agents' websites (not realizing all that information comes directly from MLS). Your house might be *the one*, but buyers will only find it *if* it's priced right. If the price is too far outside the correct range, they won't see it until you reduce the price. And if you reduce the price too late, those buyers will be gone. Market conditions can change, and not always for the better.

Most sellers don't want to believe this.

This is why pricing your home right in the beginning is key for attracting the most buyers when the listing goes active on the market. Having more buyers in the beginning will bring the highest offer. The goal when listing your home is to get *instant activity* and buyers viewing your property. The more interested buyers, the more competition, and the higher the price you'll get for your home.

CRITICAL DECISION: The *Price is Right* is not just a game show. If you go shopping for a high-ticket item or even another home, you *know* when the price is right or if it's out of whack. It's the same with every buyer interested in your home. If you price it wrong, you'll be the one paying the difference in price reductions, with your home sitting on the market longer than it should.

If you want to get buyers to make offers, use the strategy that works. Price it right. Here is some pricing data you should know:

- Overpricing your home will only bring in 2-5 percent of buyers, and most will expect a price reduction.
- Pricing right at, or slightly under market value, will bring in 80 percent of buyers.
- Pricing too low will bring in 50 percent of buyers who might bid up the price, but usually not as high as

market value. Many buyers will pass it by because they think the low price means the house has issues.

Other homes will come on the market and sell quicker if they are priced right, making your home look even more overpriced — something many sellers don't think about. Most buyers don't like to make offers on overpriced homes and are often willing to wait for price reductions. Buyer agents will also do a market analysis for their clients before the buyer makes an offer using the same market data your listing agent used to complete your market analysis. All the experts use MLS. Remember this:

- A cash buyer willing to overpay is like finding a needle in a haystack.
- If you get no showings, that means the house is overpriced.
- If you get showings without offers, that means the house is overpriced.

You may say, "Wait, Michelle, I've been looking at houses too! I know what the average market prices are right now."

Even if this is true, you've been looking for the home *you* want to buy. You've also most likely been looking for the most expensive homes in the area that you think are comparable to yours because you want the highest price in your sale. You're not looking at lower-priced homes that may be more like yours. You are biased. It's normal. Instead, you need to trust the information the market, and your listing agent, are giving you.

As a reminder, here is what not to do when trying to price your home:

- Don't use Zillow.com to do a market analysis.
- Don't base your home price on your neighbor's price.
- Don't think you'll get more for an overly customized home, as they often sell for less than comparable homes.
- Don't price based on what you "need" to sell the house for because buyers don't care.
- Don't price your home on emotional attachment.
- Don't pretend you don't know when you are overpricing your home.
- Don't look for the one agent who gives you a list price higher than others. If you receive two or three similar prices and then one that's a lot higher, look at the market data that listing agent has provided because something is out of whack. They are probably just overpricing to get you to sign the listing so they can use your property as a billboard to get more clients (as I mentioned earlier).

It's also important to think about the cost of letting your house sit on the market for an extended period. If you haven't priced your home correctly, the mental, physical, and financial costs can include:

- Constant cleaning for showings.
- Outdoor upkeep, plowing, or shoveling in winter.
- If the house is vacant, paying for utility bills and damage from storms.

- Monthly bills, taxes, and insurance.
- Managing pest infestations.
- Unintended insurance losses while the house is vacant as a result of frozen plumbing or a break-in.

Letting your listing agent do their job and use their knowledge, resources, and market data to develop a strategic listing price is one of the best ways to reach your goal of selling your home for top dollar. Trust me, buyers are waiting for your home, and every home will sell *at the right price.*

FACTORS THAT AFFECT YOUR HOME'S LISTING PRICE

Aside from the pricing trends in the local market, here are four other factors that play a key role in how much you'll be able to sell your home for.

Factor #1: Location

Even though having the same street address won't guarantee you the same price your neighbor sold their home for, your location is an important factor when setting the price for your home. Consider these things:

- **Proximity to local amenities.** There's a big difference between a five-minute drive to the nearest grocery store or school and a 20-minute drive. Where your house is located in your town or city will be a critical detail to consider.

- **Surrounding environment.** Is your house across the street from a factory or at the end of a cul-de-sac? Does your house sit on the most spacious lot in the neighborhood or is it the smallest lot next to the busy corner?
- **Accessibility.** Is your driveway flat or on a hill? Is there ample parking? New Hampshire is the Granite State, so residents are used to the driveways with hills and backyards with steep drop-offs, but out-of-state buyers might be put off by this.

Factor #2: Condition

You might have the best location, but if your roof is 30 years old and your kitchen and bathrooms haven't been updated in 25 years, that affects the price. Buyers often prefer not to do work themselves, and if they think there are many repairs needed, they may walk away or offer you less money. Even though there are loans specifically for people who are fixing up a home, many buyers aren't handy or just need to move in once they close.

Big ticket items to consider are the roof, heating system, central AC, well and septic, if any, and the condition of the walls and paint. Similarly, even if your home is impeccably clean with a new furnace and central AC, if the interior is dated, that will impact what buyers are willing to pay.

You'll also need to consider the condition of your flooring. Do you have hardwood, linoleum, or engineered hardwood? Hardwood is timeless. If you have hardwood floors under carpet, that's a value-add because people love hardwood. However, if you have different flooring materials or colors from room to room, buyers may not like that. And wall-to-wall carpet is a disappointment for those with allergies. Flooring is tricky because it's hard to change once you've moved in. If a buyer thinks they'll need to redo the flooring, they may pass on your house or offer less because replacing the flooring is a big job that may need to be done before moving in.

Basically, the less work that's needed to bring your home up-to-date, the more money you can make. Remember Plans A, B, and C that I created for Mike and Lauren? This is the point in the process where you'll have conversations with your listing agent about priorities to decide what is worth fixing and what isn't. No matter what you choose, your listing agent is there to help you make decisions that maximize your sale price.

It's important to know that when it comes to improvements, like updating a bathroom or repainting walls, buyers often overestimate or double the cost of what it would actually take to finish the project. For example, if updating a bathroom will cost you $6,000, the buyer may think it will cost $12,000. This is true about most updates a home might need. The problem is that things are much more expensive now compared to 10 years ago. If your walls are dingy and it costs you $5,000 to paint them, buyers may think it will cost $10,000. This can lead them to discount the home's value. But if you paint them, you will get a higher selling price from a larger number of buyers.

As I write this book, roofs are a big insurance issue. Insurance companies are using drones to look at the condition of roofs and may insist on a roof replacement even if the roof is between 10–20 years old and in good shape (crazy, right?). Be advised that your roof might be something you need to replace to get your home sold.

The less work a buyer must do to your home to update or repair its condition, the larger the number of interested buyers you'll get, leading to maximum price offered for your home. Still, time is money, and not all sellers have either to work with.

Also, if the home is in the starter-home range, you need to make sure it's fully functional. Many starter-home buyers barely have money for closing, let alone to purchase and fix things. So, don't spend their money for them. They just want to close, move right in, then make adjustments over time. By leaving work to do, you make the buyer conjure up high costs in their head. Instead, you want to make it easy for them to say yes to buying your home. The more complete and ready-to-go your home is, the easier the yes will be, and the more value it will have for more buyers. It will appraise better as well, making it easier for buyers to get a loan.

Keep in mind that even if you're willing to do some work to update your house, but your habit is to buy things cheap or used, you're not likely to get the most value for your home when you sell. If the work is not professional-looking, buyers will not pay for the updates because they'll want to rip them out after closing and redo them. If you've repainted the house, but it doesn't look professional, buyers will see the work and question why you did it in the first place. Sometimes, it's better not to do anything at all than to do it poorly. So, when you're redoing your house before a sale, make sure it's quality work. Cheap work will lead to lower offers. The more you think, *Cheap, cheap, cheap,* as you're making updates, the more you're going to get cheap, cheap, cheap in your offer.

Let your agent be your professional guide to what needs to be done. If you're flipping a house, that's a different situation. But for a homeowner trying to update their home to sell for top dollar, quality work is key.

> When you're redoing your house before a sale, make sure it's quality work. Cheap work will lead to lower offers.

My recommendation is to reach out to a listing agent well before you're ready to list your property so you can get professional input on what you should fix before putting it on the market. Don't make any changes or fixes before consulting your listing agent. If you do it the wrong way, you could spend money on unnecessary things. Your listing agent can help you prioritize what's important, no matter your budget.

Factor #3: Time of Year (Seasons and Weather)

There's never a bad time to sell. There are buyers in the market even throughout the holidays, but often fewer homes on the market. If you're ready to sell at that time, list your house. People need to sell and move for various reasons, whether it's work-related, family-related, a death, a divorce, a new family member, engagement, or marriage. For the same reasons you need to sell, others need to buy. Even during the holidays, though there might be fewer homes on the market, there are still buyers looking. Sellers often struggle with thinking it's not a great time of year to sell, and depending on the location of your property, some seasons might be a challenge due to weather, but all things considered, buyers are out all year long.

Don't get caught up by thinking, *Oh, my home's in New Hampshire. It's October, and winter's coming. It's not a great time to sell. There won't be any buyers. I'll wait until spring, even if waiting means the house will sit vacant.*

Don't wait.

Put your house on the market.

There are buyers out there who will want your house. Price it right, and it will sell. You don't want the carrying costs of a New England winter like paying for fuel and electricity or worrying about a tree crashing through the roof during a snowstorm or ice storm. Even if you don't live in New England, there are many reasons you don't want to have an empty house, especially during the winter.

Factor #4: Marketing

This is probably the most critical factor for attracting the right buyers in the shortest amount of time for the highest offer. The way your listing agent markets your property is how your home is presented to the world. Yes, *the world.* Anyone who has internet can see your home for sale online. Don't let your agent minimize this fact. If the marketing is not done well, your house will already have a handful of strikes against it in the buyer's mind before they even step foot through your front door.

For example, if there are some unflattering cosmetic issues in your house and your agent takes marketing pictures that only show the most picturesque angles, potential buyers will feel the property has been misrepresented when they arrive for a showing and will likely lose interest in your home even if the price or availability changes in the future.

Remember that if your home is priced right based on location and condition, the marketing is what will make or break the deal. In Chapter 6, I've outlined all the best practices for marketing and showings so you can attract the right buyers. Good marketing, at a high level, will have:

- High-quality photos that are light and bright.
- Shows the entire property in a way that buyers feel like they've walked through it.
- Accurately represents the condition of the home, even if there are issues.

SELLING YOUR HOUSE AS-IS

Sometimes sellers ask me, "What if I can't do anything? I just need to sell the home as it is." I've run into this recently, and I'll start off by saying it's absolutely okay. A good agent will work with your situation, whatever it is. If you're reading this and feel overwhelmed or think that you can't make any changes and quickly need to sell for top dollar because you have another situation to manage — maybe it's an ailing parent, or you just can't physically manage the work — I get it. In these scenarios, pricing your home accurately is the number one thing we need to focus on.

Your agent can provide resources and strategies to come up with a solid plan to clear the home for showing its best. When

I'm working as the listing agent in these cases where my client needs to sell as-is, I start by assessing all their home's positive attributes. We go through what needs to be noted in your Property Disclosure document and highlight the positives. If your home is cluttered — maybe the bedroom is full of clothes, or the spare room became the storage area, and the basement is full — that's okay. I've seen it all. I have connections for donations and a list of people who can help. Most agents have at least a short list of resources if they've been in the business for a while. Life is overwhelming for many people, and I'm never going to think poorly of my clients.

Whatever your situation, you'll work through the details with your agent to make the house look its best. Be sure to discuss your need or desire to sell as-is (and be honest about what "as-is" looks like in your home) before you sign a listing agreement with your agent, and be sure that agent is eager to help you with all the right resources to get your home presented in the best light.

This is why it's important to talk to agents before you hire one. Ask them, "How can you help me?" In times when a home needs more than a little TLC, you need an expert on your side. You don't want an agent who will take the listing, snap a few pictures while there's clutter everywhere, and leave it at that.

It often surprises sellers just how much the listing agent does to help them get the most money for their home. If your home is not in great condition, don't worry — many homes aren't. There is always a way to get your home sold.

KEYS TO A SUCCESSFUL SALE

1. The buyer, not the seller, determines a home's value. Agents analyze local comps, market trends, and your property's condition to set a fair listing price. Overpricing often leads to wasted time, price reductions, and fewer qualified offers.

2. A prime location won't bring top dollar for a house needing major repairs or updates. Tackle necessary fixes, present the home honestly, and let a professional agent handle high-quality photos, listings, and showings to attract serious buyers.

3. Concealing defects or omitting facts can sink a sale. Honest disclosures, strategic professional upgrades, and pricing a home well for its location and condition can ensure a smoother transaction with the highest possible return.

CHAPTER 5

UNDERSTANDING THE LISTING AGREEMENT AND SETTING YOURSELF UP FOR SUCCESS

"Why does every agent I meet want me to sign a listing agreement instantly? It's like we talk for five minutes, and suddenly, they're asking me to sign. We talk for another hour, and they're still asking me to sign. Sometimes, I feel like I should sign just because they spent an hour with me."

This is such a common experience that I hear from sellers, and it's incredibly unfortunate. Selling a home is one of the most emotional and stressful times in a person's life. It could be that sellers are just moving on to something better, but sometimes there's a lot of emotion running high, like with a divorce situation, a property tied up in debt, or an estate sale.

It's emotionally hard to sell a home, period. Still, even in those moments, you need to be intentional about who you choose to work with to sell your house.

Some agents know just what to say to get the listing agreement signed, but they don't follow through after getting the listing. Some agents aren't comfortable with the huge task but are nice and kind, and sellers feel bad for taking their time, so they sign out of a sense of obligation. If sellers are totally stressed and not thinking clearly, they can feel pressured to sign a listing agreement they might not have agreed to under different circumstances. If you don't think you'll be able to make a logical decision when meeting with agents, I recommend having a trusted friend present with you when you set up appointments to meet with listing agents.

So, why is it so hard to talk to a listing agent without feeling that pressure? Because that's how the real estate industry is designed. Agents are trained to get the contract signed immediately — on the spot — before the seller changes their mind. It's a tactic that's been taught for years and years. Kind of like buying a car; it's a competitive situation, and no agent wants to walk away and lose the deal. So many agents are coached on how to get signed contracts, but there's very little training about the customer service end of real estate. They're great at convincing sellers to sign the listing agreement, but they aren't great at marketing and getting the listing sold for top dollar.

Some agents are committed to helping their clients, and some agents only think of each client as a paycheck. I always feel bad for the client when I see this type of behavior.

Drop a pin anywhere on a map — especially in affluent areas — and you'll find tons of Realtors buzzing around, eager for listings. The moment they hear about a potential seller, they're trained to swoop in to be the first through the door to get a signed contract. It's unfortunate, but some agents only set goals for signing contracts instead of working in the seller's best interest, which only becomes clear once the paperwork has been signed. You can see this by looking online at the way listing agents present properties in MLS. Bad photos, missing information, and not making it easy for buyers to view the property are all telltale signs. You could probably find 10 active listings right now if you wanted to.

What's even more unfortunate is that many of those agents don't understand what it truly means to help people. They don't think beyond "get the listing." That's where a black hole exists. Sellers sign agreements and later feel frustrated because their agent isn't doing the job they promised.

How often have you heard about someone having a bad experience with a listing agent? I wish I could say it wasn't common, but it is. Those agents not only fail their clients but also give the entire industry a bad reputation. Unfortunately, those experiences stick with people, shaping how they view all agents.

This is why a listing agreement is so important. While it's easy for sellers to feel overwhelmed or pressured by a bad agent, the listing agreement is actually a powerful contract that can be used as a tool for setting expectations

> While it's easy for sellers to feel overwhelmed or pressured by a bad agent, the listing agreement is actually a powerful contract that can be used as a tool for setting expectations and safeguarding seller interests.

and safeguarding seller interests. In this chapter, I'll guide you through key components and customization options in your listing agreement to ensure you're protected and fully informed before committing to any agent.

PROTECTING YOUR INTERESTS WITH A STRONG LISTING AGREEMENT

Once you think you've found the right listing agent for your home, it's time to sign a listing agreement. The listing agreement is a legally binding contract between the seller and the listing agent and their brokerage, outlining the terms and responsibilities of both parties. While many agents treat it as a standard formality, it's important to know you can customize the agreement to better protect your interests. For example, you can include specific terms in the listing agreement, such as:

- **Availability.** Define agent and seller availability for showings and set clear boundaries to avoid disruptions. Remember to make your home as available as possible to allow the most buyers in, especially during the first few weeks.
- **Open houses.** Specify if, when, and who will conduct open houses, whether it's your listing agent or another agent if your agent isn't available. Don't forget that the other agent may not be able to represent your property and might only be able to represent buyers.

- **Photography standards.** Request that photos accurately reflect the home's current condition and season (e.g., change snow-covered yard photos when spring comes). Be sure your agent is willing to change photos if they are not great quality or not attracting the right buyers. Agents should also not reuse photos when re-listing a property.
- **Marketing expectations.** Outline expectations around marketing the property, including online listings, flyers, and social media. If your agent is resistant to certain marketing efforts, and you haven't actually signed the agreement yet, it could be a red flag.
- **Communication.** Set clear expectations for how and when you wish to receive updates from your listing agent. This could include weekly updates via email or twelve to twenty-four-hour response time to all calls, texts, or emails, feedback on showings (when provided), and weekly updates on market conditions.

By including these terms, you hold the agent accountable for delivering the level of service you expect. I have an online list of additional items you might consider at CriticalDecisionsBooks. com/Resources.

When the contract doesn't clearly define expectations, the agent has full control. They may take the listing, do as little as possible, and leave the seller stuck in an agreement until it expires. Unsold homes can remain on the market until the listing contract runs out. No seller wants their listing to "expire" before the home sells. Sometimes though, the seller is to blame. A difficult seller can really impede progress on getting a home sold, so don't be unreasonably difficult if you truly want to get your home sold.

By including clear stipulations in the listing agreement, you gain the ability to hold your agent accountable. If they fail to meet agreed-upon terms — like not communicating as agreed or failing to update listing details — you may have grounds to terminate the agreement. For instance, if four weeks have passed and you haven't heard from your agent, or your agent hasn't uploaded better listing photos, you can reference the contract and have a direct conversation with your agent. If your agent still doesn't meet their obligations, you may need to escalate to the managing broker and request termination.

While this process isn't always simple — and it's not something I encourage as a first course of action — it's your right as a seller to ensure you're receiving the proper services when you hire a listing agent to get your home sold. That is the expectation, and anything short of that (as long as you, the seller, have been reasonable to work with as well) should be brought forward and discussed in a *timely and professional* manner. Talk to your agent or their brokerage, if necessary, but don't wait it out.

CRITICAL DECISION: It's your right as a seller to ensure you're receiving the proper services when you hire a listing agent to get your home sold. That should be the expectation. Anything short of that (as long as you, the seller, have been reasonable to work with as well) should be brought forward and discussed in a *timely and professional* manner. Talk to your agent or the brokerage if necessary, but *don't wait it out.*

THE SELLER'S ROLE IN THE LISTING AGREEMENT

Just as the agent has responsibilities, so does the seller. If you're not fulfilling your obligations — such as keeping the home ready for showings, making it accessible to buyers, or stepping out during showings — it can strain the agent's ability to sell your home effectively.

For example, an agent might struggle to market a home if the seller delays preparing it for photos or denies showings due to constant scheduling conflicts. Although it's rare for an agent to "fire" a client, it can happen if the seller makes the process unworkable.

Again, a way to prevent these issues is to be sure you discussed timing with your listing agent and to decide you are 100 percent committed to selling your home.

PRICING AND STRATEGY CONVERSATIONS

The listing agreement also includes the home's price, which is a critical factor in the agent's ability to do their job. I detailed everything you need to know about pricing in Chapter 4, so go back and reread that chapter if you need a refresher. If you, as a seller, are unrealistic about the price and unwilling to adjust, it can create a situation where your house sits on the market for a long time. A good listing agent will have honest conversations about pricing strategy from the beginning, including a plan for if the property doesn't sell at the initial asking price. Holding onto an incorrect price will cause you to receive less in the long run. I call it the pendulum effect. The farther you pull away from the middle, the more it will swing in the opposite direction and the lower of an offer you'll get in the end.

SUCCESSFULLY NEGOTIATING YOUR LISTING AGREEMENT

Remember that your listing agreement is a contract, and the contract isn't set in stone until you and your listing agent have both signed on the dotted line. Until that happens, all the terms and conditions are open for negotiation.

If you've followed the advice I gave you in Chapters 2 and 3 for finding a quality listing agent who is aligned with your goals for the sale of your home and doesn't raise any red flags, there's a good chance the standard listing agreement they bring to the table may have some additional details I covered at the beginning of the chapter. How do I know this? Because the listing agreement I use with my clients puts our working relationship front and center, the seller not only gets the best price for their home but ensures both parties have a good experience throughout the process.

Just note that even if you feel confident that you're investing in a high-quality listing agent, it's your responsibility to review all details of your listing agreement.

DISCLOSE, DISCLOSE, DISCLOSE

The last listing document you'll need to fill out is the Property Disclosure form. This multi-page form tells prospective buyers about all the important systems in your home and any repairs, renovations, and upgrades you're aware of. This form becomes part of the Purchase and Sale Agreement (P&S) the buyer must read and sign when they make an offer. Sellers are supposed to fill out the Property Disclosure form on their own, but listing agents can answer questions to help them.

If a seller asks, "Do I really have to disclose that?" or says, "We had an issue over here, but can you not tell the buyers?" my answer is always the same: as a seller, you must disclose any defects or problems you know of or repaired because you are legally liable if a buyer finds out later. You don't want to understate the age of your furnace and then have the inspector find it's twice as old. It may cost you because when the buyers made their offer, it was based on what you told them in your Property Disclosure form. These disclosures are a critical element of developing a strong listing price and accurate listing description for your home.

If you want to misrepresent your property, I cannot represent you. You need to honestly represent property as it is. If you don't know how to answer a question on the Property Disclosure form, like if the roof was installed by the prior owner, you'll put "unknown" or "n/a." If you're not going to fix known issues, or if you already have an estimate for repairs, just be honest about this with buyers. Accurate information builds trust, and that's how you attract the best buyers.

For example, if there's a stain on the ceiling from a past leak and it's not listed in the disclosures, buyers may assume you're hiding other issues. But if you include a note that says, "Stain on ceiling from when upstairs sink leaked, was repaired with no further issues," you've eased their mind and built trust. Lack of trust means no offers — or lower offers. Every home has merits, whether it's location, features, or charm, and we need to showcase those while being upfront about the home's issues or upgrades that were identified or made in the last five to 10 years. Most homes have some.

Disclosures also become part of the marketing for your home. Your listing agent can upload your disclosures into MLS, which is helpful because buyers want to see information about the home so they can decide whether they want to view it. I recently had two showings where the agents hadn't shared the disclosures online, but the rest of the listing information looked promising. The listing agents made us schedule appointments (in the freezing cold), and upon arrival, each listing agent made us tour the *entire* property. It was long, drawn-out, and *unnecessary.* My buyer didn't like either property and would have known that if we'd seen the seller's Property Disclosure form online. It was torture and a waste of time. Marketing is important, and the information in your Property Disclosure document is part of the marketing.

Over the years, I've been shocked by agents who allow missing information or misrepresent properties through misleading photos or incomplete information in MLS. For example, I recently worked with a buyer interested in a multi-family property that had been on the market for more than two hundred days. The listing agent couldn't provide basic expense information for the rentals and instead listed tax info from two years prior.

Misinformation frustrates buyers and their agents and wastes everyone's time. Some listing agents think *I need to get every single buyer in to see the house.* When they only need to get *interested* buyers in to see the home through a good price and marketing. Attracting the wrong buyer is not good for the listing and will frustrate the seller if no offers are coming in. It's not the buyer's job to dig for accurate information — it's the listing agent's responsibility to provide it. If a buyer gets to the point of securing a mortgage and finds the tax numbers or other data are incorrect, the deal can fall apart, leaving the seller back at square one.

Accurate, honest listings are crucial. Misrepresentation is a disservice to the seller, while transparency ensures the home attracts the right buyers and leads to a successful closing. I always appreciate the professionalism of listing agents who work hard for their sellers to provide excellent marketing and honest information. When I work with buyers, those are the homes they want to make offers on. Once something in a listing raises a red flag in a buyer's eyes, it's hard to get that buyer on board to make an offer, even if they love the property.

KEYS TO A SUCCESSFUL SALE

1. A customized listing agreement can protect you and hold your agent accountable. You can add clauses on availability, communication expectations, and more, ensuring you're not stuck with an agent who isn't delivering results.

2. Your agent owes you marketing, showings, and regular updates. You owe them a home that's accessible and presentable. You both owe each other responsive and fair communication. Failing on either side stalls the sale and can lead to termination of the agreement.

3. Pricing strategy, contingency plans, and even how your agent handles open houses are all up for discussion. Stay reasonable, but don't be afraid to talk about terms that align with your goals and set you up for a successful sale at the best possible price. Your agent wants that for you as well.

CHAPTER 6

MARKETING, SHOWINGS, AND ATTRACTING THE RIGHT BUYERS

To sell your home quickly and for the best price, it's critical to repair, clean, and declutter your home before listing photos are taken. Whether that means renting a storage pod, asking friends with trucks to help move heavy items, or tackling updates like painting the interior, exterior, or porch, these preparations are essential. You might feel overwhelmed and think, *There's no way,* but I'll help you find the way. The key is making your property shine before listing it. If you need additional time to clear things out, speak with your agent about delayed showings. Once it's ready, you can focus on showings and, ideally, hosting an open house immediately after listing to attract multiple buyers.

Selling your home can feel like an inconvenience, but it's better to endure a short period of effort than to stretch it out over months. As I've said before, setting the right price and preparing your home properly will help you secure the best offers in the shortest time, reducing the stress of daily show prep and getting you closer to the sale you want. Everything you're doing now is to increase the marketability of your home. Good marketing is one of the best ways to increase buyer interest, reduce time on the market, and attract competitive offers. This chapter will cover the essential marketing channels, from traditional methods to digital outreach, and how an agent's approach can make or break the home's visibility.

SETTING THE STAGE

It's time to go, Mr. and Mrs. Seller. If you want to sell your home, most things in your closets, whether neat or messy, need to go somewhere else. You need to show a buyer that you're moving out. The more *stuff* you have in your house, the harder it is to appeal to a buyer who's willing to pay top dollar. I've seen it — buyers can sense when sellers are seriously ready to close a deal on their home and move on.

If a buyer walks into a home and feels like they could sit down and watch TV with the seller because it's so cozy, and all the seller's possessions are tucked into every corner, the seller isn't ready to go yet. A buyer won't invest in a home that doesn't feel like their own. Once you list, think of yourself as a guest. Buyers need to picture themselves moving in, not feel like strangers in someone else's space. When buyers see all your stuff, it feels too heavy for them. Many can't see beyond it, and if they think you're a pack rat, they may be wondering about the condition of your home once everything is moved out.

I know it's emotional and hard, but you and your listing agent will have a plan in place to pack, purge, or put away, and it's important to stick to it. Clear out your space. If at all possible, dated furniture and window coverings need to go. Dead plants? Lots of little decor items and trinkets? Toss, pack, or donate! A few family photos are okay, but the gallery wall of photos of your kids from newborn to adult? Pack it up. Clearing out your home is your one big job. Get going!

CRITICAL DECISION: Once you sign the listing agreement, it's time to start clearing your possessions out of the house. It's best to pretend you're not living there anymore. Decide that you're committed to the process of showing your home in the best way possible to attract the greatest number of qualified buyers who are ready to make an offer and close the deal.

If you have sliding glass doors or big windows, be sure to wipe them down or hire someone to come in and clean them. You will love what you see when they're done. So will the buyers! Clean the top edges of your drawers and cabinets. Put all the items from your junk drawer into a big box and clean out the box at night while watching your favorite show. Pack up what you're keeping, make sure the box tops close flat, and stack them in the garage, basement, or one single room.

Clean off counters, clean off the top of your refrigerator, reduce clutter in closets, and clean the bathrooms. Fix small, broken things like burnt-out lightbulbs or a cupboard door off a hinge in the kitchen. If not addressed, these details create an awful first impression with potential buyers. If you can't or don't want to tackle these projects on your own, hire someone or enlist a good friend to help. Often, other people can see things we don't because we are used to looking at them. Top dollar comes with a home that looks great as soon as you step inside. Make a good first impression, and all the hard work will have a great payoff in the quality of the offers you receive. When you see offers coming in, you'll be glad you did all the extra little things.

To learn more about renovations and staging, you can visit CriticalDecisionsBooks.com/Resources.

THE IMPORTANCE OF A STRONG MLS LISTING

I've already shared about how MLS is used by real estate agents and how every other real estate platform, like Zillow.com and Realtor.com, pulls its data from MLS. That's why it's *critical* for your listing agent to represent your property accurately in MLS.

Every detail they enter — photos, descriptions, and key features — becomes the foundation for how your property is marketed *worldwide*. Never underestimate where potential buyers will come from, and don't let your listing agent either. First impressions matter, and how your home is presented in MLS can directly impact buyer interest and offers.

For example, if your house has central AC but that detail is missing from the listing, and it's ninety-eight degrees in July, buyers might pass over your listing. If it's updated to add central AC after many buyers have already seen the listing, they may never come back and see the one small item update (it was a big deal to them, but they may never know). Ask your agent to allow you to preview your listing before it goes live in MLS. Double-check everything along with them. If something is mistakenly misrepresented, you might attract the wrong buyers or turn off the right ones. Review details, check photos, and ensure the description accurately and compellingly represents your property. You're the current owner and know the little details much better than an agent who has only been at your home a handful of times.

MLS gives us unlimited opportunities to redo items like photos, descriptions, showing instructions, etc., but your agent can *never* change dates and prices once they are entered. The original listing price is there for all agents to see and share with their clients. Agents can view the listing agent's name, and if the property expired, then came back on the market. We can even view the transaction history all the way back to the late 1990s. Because of this, if you tried to sell your house (for more than it was worth) with multiple agents and the listings expired every time, that historical information shows up for all agents to see in MLS and may possibly even be shown on sites like Zillow.com. This information makes your listing less attractive and raises questions about your current listing price. Buyers will think, *If the price was too high then, it's probably still too high now!*

Getting the details in your MLS listing correct from the beginning is critical for a successful sale. Be sure you have a flexible listing agent who will pay attention and change details if they're not working or bringing the wrong buyers. For example, I had a lakefront property with mooring spots but there was a wait list to get a mooring. The mooring attracted buyers who were excited about having a spot on the lake, but when they learned there was a wait list, they lost interest. My phone kept ringing with buyers, but we weren't getting offers. That one MLS listing detail was attracting the wrong buyers. I adjusted the MLS listing, removed any mention of the mooring, and began attracting buyers who valued the property for other reasons.

> Getting the details in your MLS listing correct from the beginning is critical for a successful sale.

This kind of responsiveness ensures a seller receives offers in the shortest amount of time. If I'd left the mooring information in the listing, the house would have sat on the market for months longer than it did. To sell quickly, listings must attract the right buyers.

Unfortunately, some agents adopt a "set it and forget it" mentality. They put the listing in MLS and never check it, make updates, or improve its appeal. You've seen those listings. Those agents will do the same to your listing if you hire them. It's their habit. But that approach can cause a property to sit on the market without attracting the right buyers.

As agents, our job is to get the MLS information correct in the beginning, market effectively, and adjust as needed — while always being truthful and ensuring accuracy. Some agents never change the listing details but will tell sellers it's time for a price reduction. This is not fair to you, the seller, and doesn't help you maximize the offers you'll receive for your property.

Details matter, and the right listing agent will be meticulous in getting your property details correct from the outset, presenting your property in the best possible light. If you want more information about finding an agent who will put in the effort to help you land top dollar for your home, visit CriticalDecisionsBooks.com/Resources.

TO HAVE AN OPEN HOUSE OR TO NOT HAVE AN OPEN HOUSE?

Years ago, open houses were primarily used for agents to attract buyers to work with. Rarely did homes sell at open houses. Since 2020, open houses have transformed into a central feature of property marketing. During the fast-paced 2020 pandemic market, a property would be listed in MLS during the week, with an open house scheduled for the upcoming weekend. Buyers would flock to the house, offers would pour in, and properties would go under contract almost immediately. This strategy still plays an important role. If a property is priced competitively, depending on location, an open house can still bring a handful of buyers who make offers

However, open houses don't always serve the seller's best interests. For instance, holiday seasons and weather play a significant role in the success of the event. Still, all it takes is one buyer, so an open house might be worth it if it's convenient for the seller. However, holding open houses repeatedly on the same property can make a property appear stale. Buyers expect open houses to draw crowds, so if a property has multiple open houses, has not gone under contract, and has not had price reductions, buyers may perceive low interest or conclude that the property is overpriced. In New Hampshire, this is especially true for homes priced under a million dollars. For multi-million-dollar properties, the dynamics can differ a bit depending on time of year and location, as these listings often attract buyers a bit further away who may need more time to view the home.

I prefer hosting open houses early in the listing process to maximize exposure, gather buyer feedback, and hopefully bring a minimum of one or two offers. Open houses provide a nice opportunity to engage directly with buyers and other agents so I can gather insight for the seller. For example, I had a recent open house where several interested buyers told me how much they loved to walk around this area. The house was just off a main road, and most homes in the area were on busy roads without sidewalks. Right after the open house, I added that detail to the MLS listing details, and buyers took notice. If a seller insists on listing at a higher price (not my favorite tactic), and we have a plan in place, an initial open house can provide real-time feedback. If it generates very little interest (considering other factors just mentioned, and being sure the home looks amazing in MLS), we'll already have the plan in place to promptly adjust the price.

Finally, it's important to know who is hosting your open house. Remember my story about the agent sleeping on my couch? Sellers often don't realize that their listing agent may delegate the responsibility of an open house to another agent in the office. This can lead to issues if the hosting agent is unfamiliar with the property. I've seen situations where critical details, such as acreage, were misrepresented by an agent who wasn't the listing agent. A buyer might make an offer based on that misinformation, causing the deal to fall apart once correct information is provided.

If you're working with a designated agent, the listing agent is the only person who will have access to your full property file. If another agent holds the open house, they may only be able to represent buyers, not your home. Some sellers are not comfortable with this, but their agent never told them the truth about the situation. Ask your listing agent to explain how open houses will work, as it could be a big piece of your marketing strategy.

SHOWINGS AND MAKING STRONG FIRST IMPRESSIONS

Showings are the cornerstone of getting your home sold. The goal is to attract the most buyers who are a good fit for your home. Those are the buyers who will fall in love and make offers. It's the single most important aspect for an agent and home seller to focus on. To sell your home quickly and for the best price, it's critical to do your part to make the home showing ready and available.

Before a showing, your home needs to look its absolute best. While you don't need to set the table with fine China, everything should be as neat and clean as possible. For some sellers, this is second nature. For others — especially those with kids, pets, or busy lives — it can feel overwhelming. But remember: showings should bring offers. The quicker you get a great offer, the quicker you can stop doing showings.

For the showings themselves, you'll need to leave the house so the listing agent or buyer agent can show interested buyers around your home. Buyers need to feel and experience the home in their own way. They need to be able to picture themselves living there. A listing agent hovering or directing buyers from room to room disrupts this natural process. Buyers hate it. Buyers especially hate *assisted showings* that are guided by the listing agent when they have a buyer agent. To avoid this, I always let buyer agents do single-broker-showings and let them know I'm available for questions via calls or text when they're showing one of my listings.

Buyer's schedules are unpredictable, so it's critical that you make your home presentable and accessible as much as possible. For example, if an out-of-state buyer is in town for a day and can't see your home due to you or your listing agent's restrictions, you might lose a perfect offer. Always prioritize flexibility and maximize showing opportunities, especially during the first two to three weeks when your house is on the market and interest is highest.

To make sure your house is as available as possible, your listing agent will use tools like showing management software to allow buyer agents to schedule a time for buyers to view your home. Requiring extended notice for showings, even asking for a 24-hour notice to show, or restricting access at popular times of day when buyers might be available can really discourage interested buyers. I can't stress how much of a problem this can be for buyers.

A buyer might call your agent from the front yard where they see the "for sale" sign. If your agent is available and you have flexible showing instructions, they just might be the perfect buyer for your home. Buyers who can't get in to tour the house will just drive off, and some may never return. I've known buyers to go out "home searching" to see as many homes as possible in one day *and make an offer on their favorite that day*. Buyers do a lot of work with online searching, which means they don't set up showing ahead of time unless they have a buyer agent who is doing that for them. Instead, they drive around the area to see if it feels good, then call when they are nearby to schedule a showing. They're not being difficult; it's how some buyers think it works. They don't understand when there are delays in seeing a home people really want to sell.

Ultimately, the priority is attracting as many qualified buyers as possible early in the process. If your agent insists on limiting access, such as requiring assisted showings or being unresponsive to inquiries, it's worth reevaluating your agent. Interestingly, I see this type of restricted viewing a lot on multi-million-dollar homes. But do buyers really need Vanna White treatment? You should put away your expensive trinkets when you list the house so theft shouldn't be a concern. Letting a buyer agent show their buyers your home without your listing agent present may help your home sell that much quicker.

Some agents use the fact that they'll do assisted showings for you as a selling feature of themselves. But by now, you know that providing good marketing materials in the home, having a listing agent who's available for a call, and allowing easy access to view your home are really all you need. In southern New Hampshire, unassisted showings have been the norm for twenty years. Some listing agents in other markets don't take to it as well, but I love single-broker showings — especially when I get a call from a buyer agent with an offer for my seller!

For unique situations, like high-end or celebrity properties, more stringent qualifications may apply, but even then, accessibility remains a top priority. Buyers are unpredictable, and the perfect one can appear at any time. Remember, the longer your home sits on the market, the more it costs you. By allowing flexibility for showing times with either a buyer agent or your listing agent present, and being ready to show from day one, you improve your chances of securing the best offer quickly. If your home isn't selling right away, you need to stay flexible until it does. If it is because it's priced too high, it will wear you out and will sell for less. Always be prepared, as much as possible, to show your home until you receive a solid offer and have a fully executed P&S.

PUTTING A SIGN IN THE FRONT YARD

As I mentioned earlier, signs are an agent's personal billboard and are used more for agents to get additional business than they are likely to sell that particular home. In many instances, buyers calling the telephone number on a sign think the property is *at least* $100,000 less than its market price. It's been this way for 20 years. This is because homes can be deceiving from the outside. Trust me, even without a sign, your home will get buyers who viewed it online.

If you are considering interviewing a listing agent because you've seen their sign out in front of a home for a long while, it's because the home isn't selling. Call them. Ask detailed questions like:

- How long has the home been on the market?
- What's going on with the pricing?
- Have they had multiple price reductions?
- Why do you think the property hasn't sold yet?

If the agent answers your call (they get some points for that), use the information I gave you in Chapter 2 and watch out for the red flags in Chapter 3 as you assess their response. Even better, use the checklist I have for you at CriticalDecisionsBooks.com/ Resources. If they speak poorly about the house or the owners and blame others for why the house hasn't sold, they're not the agent for you. How do you feel when you're talking with them? If you're unsure, I recommend always listening to your gut.

Some agents love having listings and planting a sign in the ground because it puts them in contact with buyers who also need an agent to represent them. Just remember, that sign might be getting the agent busy with other clients while your home sits on the market. Worse yet, maybe the agent is getting calls and just isn't answering their phone at all. This happens more than you would think.

THE ROLE OF PHOTOGRAPHY IN MARKETING

As I mentioned in Chapter 5, once you list your property for sale with a listing agent and your house is posted in MLS, it's instantly there for the *world* to see. Because of this, it's critical that your property is represented with excellent photos as this is what will attract buyers. You want lots of activity in the first two to three weeks after listing your home, and if the photos are not well done, you'll instantly lose buyer interest.

Sadly, not all professional photos are a great representation of the property. Some agents take their own photos, and the color is off, or they show random parts of the house, like a closeup of a shower curtain and shampoo bottle, a pasta box on the table, dirty towels hanging over the shower rod, and dishes in the sink. These types of photos make buyers think less of the home, and they'll quickly click off the listing. In their mind, it's already worth less if they see photos like that. And yes, I've seen these photos in multi-million-dollar listings. You have too. Such listings end up with multiple price reductions or expire without selling.

To avoid this outcome and to have the best possible photos, your agent should either take high-quality photos or invest in a professional photographer who specializes in real estate photography and can capture high-quality images with natural editing. This is the absolute best option for getting great listing photos.

Several years back, I taught a credit class for real estate agents called *Listing Photos: the Good, the Bad, and the Ugly*. I taught agents how to use photography to show off important areas of the home. I explained and demonstrated how to enter photos in MLS for good flow by bringing buyers through the home, how to not overdo outdoor photos, and how to avoid overloading the listing with photos of any single area. I also taught color grading and lighting for agents who had cameras and showed them how to get consistency in their images.

Before drones became popular, I took aerial real estate photos from a helicopter. Drone photography has its place but is not always done well — especially when it gives a false perspective of the home's location. If you show the lake in the drone photo, but the house is surrounded by trees, and there are no lake views, that's not an accurate representation of the listing. This frustrates buyers who could have found the same information using online maps.

Keep in mind that an agent who pays for professional photos may not be easy to convince that some photos aren't good for showing the listing in the best way possible, and they won't replace them. They may not even know what good marketing photos really are. Just like real estate agents, not all photographers are created equal, so the quality of the images may not represent your property in the best way possible. Recently, I saw a friend's listing for their lake home in Florida and noticed the professional photographer had taken the listing photos on a gray and cloudy day. The images are drab and don't represent the beautiful lake house well, and unfortunately, the house has been sitting on the market for months.

There is no need to deceive with real estate photography. Providing unrealistic photos is the same as being dishonest with your Property Disclosure document. When the buyer shows up to view the home, if the photos are not accurate, buyers get frustrated for having their time wasted, often saying, "I wish the house really looked like the photos." Buyers also take note of agents who do try to deceive. Bad photos and bad representation are bad marketing. It doesn't help the listing sell faster and feels more like a lie.

> **CRITICAL DECISION:** If the listing agent takes the listing photos instead of hiring a professional real estate photographer, ask how important the agent feels photography is to the listing. Their response will give you an eye-opening understanding of how the agent feels about marketing your home.

Taking listing photos requires good marketing sense, good lighting, consistency of lighting throughout the photos, staging areas of the home to reduce clutter in the photos, and knowing what buyers are looking for to be sure not to leave out important details.

EMAIL BLASTS AND THE VALUE OF AN AGENT'S NETWORK AND CONNECTIONS

When you hire a listing agent, you're effectively hiring that agent's entire network. These personal connections often result in more qualified leads and faster sales because your listing agent is speaking directly to serious buyers who might not have time to look at properties in MLS every day. Working these connections can lead to off-market sales or pre-listing interest (within MLS rules) that can generate offers before the home officially goes on the market.

To get as many eyes on a listing as possible, a great listing agent will send emails to their database, including agents and thousands of potential buyers (my database has more than ten thousand people around the US and the world). Not all buyers live where you're located but they *do* want to move where you're located. And not all buyers are checking Zillow.com or other listing platforms. You never know who is connected to whom, so it's important your agent has excellent reach and leverages their network, especially if you're selling a luxury home. Wealthy buyers want efficiency. They don't have time to scroll online for hours and truly appreciate a personal touch. They'll respond when personally notified about a home by someone they know, like, and trust, such as an agent or a friend who received the listing information.

It's also important for your agent to advertise on social media and be connected in local circles. Agent open houses or broker tours are a great way for other agents to preview new listings for their buyers. Making your property known to many people, not only buyers but their connections, is the best way to get buyer interest.

If you've set the stage, your agent created a strong listing with high-quality photos, you've made your home available for showings, and your agent has marketed your home correctly and leveraged their network, and you're *still* not getting interested, qualified buyers, you have a pricing problem. Go back and reread Chapter 4 and have another honest conversation with your agent about setting an accurate market price.

KEYS TO A SUCCESSFUL SALE

1. To sell quickly for top dollar, get everything ready upfront — cleaning, decluttering, repairs, etc. Quality photos, an accurate MLS listing, and a strong marketing push are essential to attract the right buyers fast.

2. Make your home easy to show, and be sure your agent is easy to reach. Restrictive or outdated listing details, complicated showing rules, or a non-responsive agent can scare off motivated buyers and lead to price reductions and take longer to get to closing.

3. A proactive agent leverages marketing blasts and personal connections and carefully vets potential buyers. If setbacks arise, they handle them quickly, professionally, and strategically to keep your listing fresh and appealing.

CHAPTER 7

THE OFFERS
ARE COMING

You did it! You finally have an interested buyer (or buyers) making an offer to buy your house! All the work that went into finding the right agent, setting the correct listing price, excellent marketing, preparing your home for showings, and relying on your agent to do whatever it takes has paid off.

This is another moment in the process when it's easy to let emotions take over. It's exciting, scary, stressful, and brings up a lot of feelings, but try to listen to your agent. Your agent is your logical guide with a clear head and a clear path to reach your goals, and they will help you avoid potential pitfalls. They'll gather details about the buyer's situation and finances, then scrutinize all other details of the offer before explaining the pros and cons of each section to you and how it affects the overall offers. Ask as many questions as you need to understand the offer your agent is presenting you.

Remember that not all buyers (or offers) are created equal.

Just because someone is interested in buying your home doesn't mean they're truly qualified. You need a buyer who can successfully complete the transaction — not someone whose offer will fall apart. As listing agents, it's our job to read between the lines, analyze the details of offers, and ask probing questions about the buyer's qualifications. For instance, a buyer might need to sell another property before completing the purchase, but they may not disclose that upfront. Deals can fall apart for numerous reasons, and the worst-case scenario for a seller is accepting an offer that falls apart before closing.

Why is a deal falling apart the worst-case scenario? Once a property goes under contract, its status in MLS changes from "active" to "active under contract" or "pending." This status shift signals to the market that the property is no longer fully available. If the contract falls apart before closing, the property returns to the market as "back on market" and always seems to raise red flags for potential buyers.

Even if the issue isn't the seller's fault, buyers may assume something is wrong with the property. This stigma can affect the property's perceived value and make it harder to sell at the original price. If I ever encounter this situation, I immediately reach out to any interested parties to secure a new contract before changing the listing status in MLS. If we can get the house back under agreement with another qualified buyer, the MLS status stays the same, keeping the integrity of the listing status in check. This must be a quick move — and why it's so important to attract a lot of qualified buyers right away — as status changes need to happen within two business days in MLS.

If you only receive one offer, it needs to be really solid before you accept it. Rely on your agent to be logical and help you vet the offer's quality. I know an offer is hard to walk away from, but if there are red flags, it may be best to wait for another offer.

If you receive multiple offers, the highest-priced offer may not be the best one. Sometimes, buyers with red flags will make the highest offer, hoping you will overlook any shortcomings. However, if you've received multiple offers, there are ways your agent can negotiate to find the best offer. It takes some finesse for sure, and not all agents like multiple offer situations (I love them), but it's absolutely critical to go through the details of each offer to find the best one for you. Don't worry about being confused; your agent will discuss the strong and weak points of every offer and how to respond to buyers strategically and thoughtfully. This is a critical step in coming to terms with the right buyer and getting to a smooth, successful closing.

KEY COMPONENTS OF AN OFFER

While cash offers can be very appealing at the beginning, you need to know what the buyer's *real* situation is. Are they saying it's a cash offer, then applying for a loan in the background? Do they have a home to sell they aren't disclosing up front? Is their money tied up for a certain length of time before they can use it? I've seen all these scenarios happen.

Cash offers can be great, but sometimes, they come with surprises that pop up after buyer and seller are under contract.

A strong offer with solid buyers who need financing but have already gone through the underwriting process with their lender can be solid buyers as well. You don't want to accept an offer from buyers who cannot prove how they are paying for the home. You want proof of funds or financing upfront. If they have excuses for not providing proof, your agent shouldn't let you sign. Wait until they have proof. Many mortgage companies work weekends and can provide pre-approvals for their buyers in an instant.

Your agent will know the differences between the types of pre-approvals and help you understand which is the best. Again, not all proof of funding or loan is created equal. Your listing agent will review and should be able to identify which banks and mortgage companies are reputable and easy to work with. Sometimes, big banks without actual offices or online lenders can be a headache at closing time. I have been in situations where big banks don't provide funding on time, or it comes in at the very last minute and makes everyone sit on eggshells, waiting to see if the deal is going to close on time.

Many sellers mistakenly assume that once the contract is signed, the hard work is over, but the path to closing is rarely straightforward. A successful closing depends heavily on your agent managing each stage of the process from contract to closing.

Once an offer is accepted by the seller and signed by the buyer and seller, it is *fully executed* and becomes a legally

> Many sellers mistakenly assume that once the contract is signed, the hard work is over, but the path to closing is rarely straightforward.

binding agreement. This is often referred to as a Purchase and Sale Agreement (P&S), contract, or offer. Essentially, the contract acts as the guide for the transaction and timeline. There are important clauses and dates outlined within the contract that guide the process to closing, and these are critical to track. Here are some of the most common elements of a P&S:

- **Price.** This is usually what sellers feel is most important, but other details of the contract must be strong, along with the price.
- **Deposit Amount.** This often shows the buyer's level of seriousness to the seller.
- **Offer Amount.** This amount, less any concessions on the final page of the contract, is what the buyers are offering to pay for your home.
- **What is Included.** This could be a simple list of appliances or very specific items requested by the buyer. Both parties need to agree for this list of items to be included in the sale.
- **Inspections.** The buyer pays for inspections. It's best to complete inspections as soon as possible.
- **Payment Method.** Is the buyer paying with cash or financing? No matter the method, get proof of funds or pre-approval.
- **Commitment Date.** With a loan, this is when the buyers are officially approved for the loan. Hopefully, the lender or buyer agent has told the buyers not to buy a car, take out another loan, or quit their job before closing, or their financing can fall apart.

- **Buyer Request for Seller Paid Buyer Agent Fees.** This would have been a conversation you had with your agent when you signed the listing agreement.
- **Buyer Request for Seller Paid Closing Costs.** This is commonly requested when buyers are financing with a low down payment and don't have a lot of additional funds to meet all closing costs.
- **Contingencies and Clauses.** Every situation is different. You want your listing agent to be strong in this area to get you to a smooth closing. Some contracts have no contingencies or clauses; others have several. Poorly written clauses in a contract can create problems as the contract progresses. My first manager was instrumental in helping me learn how important clause language is.

  I once received an offer where a buyer agent gave up and had the buyers write the list of contingencies themselves because they were *driving her crazy.* How scary is that? In the end, the sellers did not accept the offer.
- **Closing Date.** This is the date everyone is waiting for. Your home is officially sold! You receive a check, and the buyer receives the keys. Certain days of the week are better for closings than others.

You can learn more about the important details included in a Purchase and Sale Agreement on my website at CriticalDecisionsBooks.com/Resources.

Real estate agents in New Hampshire use a standard P&S, and today's technology allows buyers and sellers to sign with just a few taps on their phone or computer. Deposits can be made online, as wire payments eliminate the need for checks. The title company or attorney has specific procedures to make sure it is all done legally, so no checks or deposits should ever be made out directly to an agent, seller, or buyer when working with real estate agents. The buyer's deposit goes into escrow and is held by the listing agent's brokerage or buyer agent's brokerage.

If a transaction falls apart, it is not in the listing agent or buyer agent's control to release the deposit in escrow. Both the buyer and seller must sign off on a deposit release — a process that is also covered by a specific set of guidelines. There are specific regulations and guidelines that must be followed for any money exchanged in a real estate transaction.

TITLE COMPANIES, ATTORNEYS, AND CLOSINGS (OH, MY!)

My clients, Ruth and Louie, were selling one property and using the funds from that sale to buy another. The buyers of their home, Karl and Sandra, were closing with an attorney instead of a title company. The moving truck arrived early on the day of closing. I had Ruth and Louie sign their paperwork the day before, so all they needed was to load the truck and head to close on their purchase. Karl and Sandra signed their papers in the morning, and the only thing left to do was for Karl and Sandra to call their attorney's office to confirm Ruth and Louie had moved out. Everything was lined up perfectly.

In the days leading up to the closing date, I checked and double-checked with all parties involved and knew Karl and

Sandra just had to call their attorney before the wire cutoff time to get the money sent to the title company. Same-day wires can be tricky because they are not guaranteed, but they are done all the time. Ruth and Louie left with the moving truck to go to the closing, but Karl and Sandra were nowhere to be found! They weren't answering calls from me or their attorney. Ruth and Louie's closing all rested on Karl and Sandra calling the attorney to release the funds!

Forty-five minutes later, Karl and Sandra arrived. They were walking around, talking, and taking their time going through their new home. I tried to be patient yet persistent in getting them to call the attorney to release the funds. Then, they wanted the sellers to come back and get something out of the basement before calling the attorney. I remained calm and explained the situation, and promised all would be gone later that day. It was very stressful for all involved (except Karl and Sandra). They finally made the call with moments to spare. Then, we waited for the wired funds to show up at the title company.

Just for some perspective: if both closings were at a title company or, better yet, at the same title company, this situation would have gone much smoother with no deadline and no call to an attorney. Karl and Sandra's attorney, however, would not agree to this. Their attorney's office also had an old-fashioned practice of walking over to the courthouse to record the deed by hand before manually sending the wire.

Most title companies in New Hampshire have funding accounts, and deeds are recorded electronically, expediting the process. These are important things for your agent to think through on your behalf, depending on the buyer's choice of closing location. With Ruth and Louie's buyers, I knew all the places the train could go off the track and had taken all this into consideration, lined it up with precision, and worked through the timeline multiple times with the attorney and title company beforehand. The only thing I did not have control over was Karl and Sandra being late or whether the wire would be processed and sent on the same day.

Fortunately, the wire arrived that day! Papers were signed, and Ruth and Louie closed without a hitch. If you've ever wondered, yes, there are a lot of details to manage to get to a smooth closing. Often, it's the real estate agent sweating the most, and they handle things you'll never even know could happen. Closings sure are something to celebrate!

The dates in a contract are critical details that can make or break your deal. You want a solid purchase and sales contract with tight dates, along with a listing agent who is detailed and keeps the contract on track. If the buyers fail to meet any of their dates, they're "out of contract," and you need to have an important conversation with your listing agent to see how things will progress.

QUICK OFFER, QUICK CLOSING

Why, as a seller, would you want your home to go under contract quickly and then close quickly? When you get a buyer and a contract, you might think, "Wow, that was great. I don't need to move for 90 days."

This is important to understand: when a buyer makes an offer on your home, especially if you do not have many buyers, it is better to close sooner rather than later. If you have multiple buyers making offers, the one that is strongest, with the quickest closing date, is best.

Many things can happen in people's lives. If a buyer needs financing, you and your listing agent will review the details before accepting the offer. Even if the buyers are prepared to put down a large deposit, things can still go wrong. Maybe, God forbid, one of them loses their job or has a bad accident and can't fulfill their mortgage obligation. If that happens on day 63 and you're closing in 90 days, you'll be back on the market, have to start all over, and most likely will have to sell at a lower price. If you had closed in 45 days, that issue would not have affected you.

> When a buyer makes an offer on your home, especially if you do not have many buyers, it is better to close sooner rather than later.

Let's say a buyer puts down a $100,000 deposit on your lake house in October and wants to close in April. You may be happy staying in your house all winter, but a long period between contract and closing might not be in your best interest. A lot can happen during that time.

Sure enough, a new property comes on the market in February. The buyers of your home fall in love with that other house. It's *the* house they've always wanted, and it hasn't been available in 20 years. Suddenly, they want to buy the other house.

You think, *Well, they put a deposit on my home, and they've signed a Purchase and Sale Agreement, which is a legal contract. It shouldn't be a problem, right?*

What you don't know is that money isn't an issue for your buyers. They don't care if they lose the deposit. They just want to buy the other house.

Can they do that? They can. It could become a messy court battle if you want to explore that option, but you'll still want to sell your house, and if they're not buying it, your house needs to go back on the market.

Let's say your buyers sign over the deposit for you to keep and buy the other house. You now must put your home back on the market, which could be a challenge if market conditions have worsened. It's not what you expected would happen, and it's likely that other buyers who were interested in your house back in October aren't available anymore. To add salt to the wound, you had another home you were going to purchase after the sale of this one. Sadly, you're going to have to let that fall through because of this unfortunate situation.

We agents call this the domino effect.

Yes, some buyers are willing to walk away from their deposit if they find something better. Some will fight to get their deposit back even though they no longer want to buy your house. The more time between putting a property under agreement and closing, the greater the chance for the deal to fall apart. This doesn't happen all the time, but it can. It's better to tie everything up neatly with a bow and close in the shortest amount of time possible.

If you find a solid buyer who wants to close in 20 days, do it. Figure out how to make it work. The quicker you close, the better. If you go back on the market four months later, you might be in a better market, but you might not. You could get more, or you could get less. And whether you can keep their deposit isn't always a given — it's not automatically handed to you. In New Hampshire, both the buyer and the seller must sign off for the deposit to be released to either party. If the buyer doesn't sign off, you don't automatically get the funds. That's a whole other conversation I'm happy to discuss with you at another time.

These things do happen. Buyers are fickle. They get cold feet. Their lives change.

The moral of the story is you need to sell quickly and close quickly.

KEYS TO A SUCCESSFUL SALE

1. Every offer comes with a range of factors like deposits, fees, contingencies, and closing dates that can impact how smoothly the sale proceeds. An offer with strong financing or fewer contingencies may be more valuable than a higher-priced offer that's likely to fall apart later.

2. Once you accept an offer, strict deadlines for inspection periods, financing commitments, and closing dates guide the transaction. Buyers missing deadlines can create challenges, so your listing agent must track them closely to keep the deal moving forward.

3. Leaving a long gap between "going under contract" and closing on your home can invite buyer uncertainty and raise the chances of a deal collapsing. Buyers may find another property or face personal setbacks. Tying up the sale quickly helps avoid these pitfalls and ensures you get your money sooner.

CHAPTER 8

SELLING TO BUY

If you're selling your home and buying a new one at the same time, you're not alone. Many sellers plan to use the sale proceeds from their current house for a new house. However, a mistake many excited buyers make is diving into house hunting before understanding the value of their current home. Being logical as a buyer is just as important as being logical as a seller. Knowing what you can sell your current house for is essential to making a good buying decision. This chapter provides essential guidance for homeowners navigating this dual process.

WHEN YOUR LISTING AGENT IS ALSO YOUR BUYER AGENT

Sometimes, I'll talk with a client who comes to me as a buyer, but they're also a seller because they need to sell to buy. Selling to buy is different from buying first and *then* selling your home. If a seller has enough resources, cash, or the ability to get a loan, buying a new home before selling their current one is a nice option because they can move out and empty the current home, make sure it shows well, then sell it. This takes the stress off closing on two homes on the same day and having all your possessions sitting in a moving truck to move from house to house.

The biggest advantage to buying before you sell is that you don't have a Sale of Home contingency in your offer. That contingency will weaken even the best offer because sellers generally don't like to accept an offer with a Sale of Home contingency. Some will, especially if the price and terms are reasonable, but just know that if a seller accepts your offer with a Sale of Home contingency, they may give you a short window — maybe 30 days — to get your current home under contract. After that, your offer to buy may become null and void. That is only one example, as each contingency is written up on a case-by-case basis to work for both the buyer and seller.

Selling your home is the key to making this happen. To begin with, you need a market analysis. A market analysis is the most important item in making this whole big picture come together. If you ask yourself, "What can I sell my house for?" a market analysis will give you everything you need to know.

If my client needs to sell to buy, I can help them best if both homes are within my area. One agent working through both contracts is most efficient for moving the process along because they're managing all the details of both transactions. If one of the homes is too far away, I can refer my client to another agent and work closely with that agent to get both homes sold for our mutual client. It's stressful for clients moving far away from the home they are selling, but having two mutually invested agents in their goals is key to a smooth process.

If money is not an issue, and you can afford to buy a home of any price, regardless of what your current one sells for, that is an ideal situation but much less common. A market analysis of your current property is crucial for establishing what you could potentially get from the sale of your home. In an analysis, your agent will also calculate what you can expect to net — the bottom line after fees and expenses, mortgage payoff, closing costs, commission, New Hampshire transfer tax, etc. Then, you'll have a dollar amount to apply toward your new home purchase.

Looking for a new home is the exciting part. It is filled with dreams and possibilities. Whereas the home to sell may be filled with personal possessions, and the thought of packing and moving can overwhelm even the most organized people. And, because it's exciting, people start there. But honestly, you'll miss your perfect house if you don't know your numbers and what you can sell your current house for.

If I ask a seller, "Do you know how much you can sell your house for?"

Most respond with, "The Zillow website says it's worth..." or "My neighbor sold for this price, so mine will definitely sell for more."

Neither statement is accurate.

The Zillow website is just data from an algorithm — a computer program that has never been inside your house. The algorithm has no idea if your home has been updated or was renovated in 2005, whether it's in excellent condition or needs some repairs. It doesn't know if your home smells like the perfume counter at Macy's, cinnamon rolls, or a barn full of cows.

The price listed on Zillow.com for your current home is often far off what the current buyers may pay, especially if you've been in your home for more than 10 years. I've seen Zillow Zestimates® that were off by $100,000 or more. Instead of relying on the Zillow website, work with a listing agent to do a market analysis so you can have a *real number* to value your home.

> **CRITICAL DECISION:** Work with a listing agent to get a market analysis on your current home before you start looking for a new house. By understanding the value of your current house, you'll have a clear idea of how much you can afford to pay for a new home. No surprises. You might *think* you know how much your home is worth, but what if that's wrong?

If I'm working with a client who is selling their home to buy another, I'll review their home and current market price, and, as I mentioned in Chapter 4, we'll talk about updates and repairs. The seller of the home you are under contract to buy will be watching your listing closely. It *must* be priced correctly. If you aren't ready to sell, a current market analysis will give you a realistic price for when the time comes to look for a new home. If too much time passes after your market analysis, have your agent do another one to be sure it is still a good price for the current market in case there've been any market changes (don't miss this step!).

If I have a listing and a buyer falls in love with it, but that same buyer needs to sell but is not ready to sell, I'll talk with my seller, but they may not accept the buyer's offer. Knowing what your home can realistically sell for will save you frustration and prevent heartbreak caused by missing out on the perfect home.

KEYS TO A SUCCESSFUL SALE

1. Work with a listing agent to do a current market analysis on your home before you start house hunting so you have a clear understanding of how much your home is worth and how much purchasing power you have.

2. If you're planning a local move, find a listing agent for your current house who can also act as your buyer's agent for your new house. This person will likely have a strong grasp of the current market and facilitate the sale and purchase of both properties within your desired timeline.

3. Experienced agents are your biggest asset. They can balance multiple transactions and successfully get you to closing. They can sense potential issues and find solutions before they arise. The right agent will be confident in managing all details and help you remain calm and focused on packing and moving. The best agents are worth their weight in gold, and can make things happen that you never thought possible.

CHAPTER 9

IT'S THE PEOPLE FIRST, THEN THE PROPERTIES

After several recent closings, I was talking with another agent, and she asked, "Did you do all the work on both sides of the transactions, or did the other agents actually help you?"

That might sound strange, but it's a valid question that those of us who work hard for our clients completely understand. When two agents are involved in a transaction — a listing agent and a buyer agent — they don't always pull equal weight. One might be highly responsive, the other, not so much. This happens because our industry is filled with people who have a real estate license but who do not work in real estate full-time. They also may not be up-to-date with critical details that can make or break a deal. Some agents don't follow up, don't attend home inspections for their clients, or don't respond right away, but those of us who care about our clients will do whatever it takes to get our clients' deals to closing.

Someday, I hope the education standards and training requirements for real estate agents are raised to reduce some of the issues I've written about in this book. I know it's a big dream, but I'm looking into ways to help it along. We can and need to do better. There are many good agents, but it would be great to give clients more certainty in their expectations of representation.

If you've ever bought or sold a home, I hope this book sheds some light on things that didn't make sense at the time. My editor recently bought a home, and even though this book is for home sellers, she said it helped her make sense of things she didn't understand at the time. If your home is not already on the market, take some time and process what I've shared. It's not only okay to spend the time to find the right agent well ahead of putting your house on the market, but it may also be the best thing to do.

Sometimes, sellers think that "everyone will know" that they met with an agent to discuss selling their home but didn't actually hire them. They're afraid they'll be blacklisted in some way, and their home won't sell. Trust me, this is untrue. As a matter of fact, most agents will not share the fact that they are meeting with you to discuss selling your home. They won't share your name or address until the listing agreement is signed for fear that another agent will steal the listing from them (yes, agents are very competitive that way). So, if you meet with an agent and don't hire them on the spot (or never), don't worry; they don't want to broadcast the fact that they didn't get the listing.

As I was writing this book and thinking about how much I care that people are well taken care of, it brought me back to some early memories I'd long forgotten about.

I was an excited six-year-old when I could *finally* reach the old-fashioned register in my family's business. My dad taught me how to make change, and my aunt taught me how to say thank you when handing it back to customers. Customer service was at the heart of everything we did. Without our customers, there would be no business. At 21, I ventured out and opened my first business, taking care of customers with all I'd learned. Ten businesses later, customers are still always at the core of what I do.

"Extreme customer service" was the tagline on my personal letterhead back in 2002 when I became a licensed real estate agent, and it's still how I take care of people who are selling their biggest assets — protecting theirs as I do my own.

What we do as real estate agents, when we're committed to our clients, is detailed and hard work. It's also very important work. There are not many industries where we get to help clients through one of the biggest financial transactions of their lives. It pains and frustrates me when I see homeowners struggling to get their homes sold with their agent, seeing bad photos in MLS or poor descriptions of beautiful properties, knowing how little their agent is working for them.

And that's why I wrote this book.

Moving can be stressful, but having the right team in place makes all the difference. Whether you're selling, buying, or doing both, be sure the agent you choose will prioritize your best interests. This makes the process less stressful and will help you feel better if any challenges arise along the way. You need someone you can count on. At the end of the day, good customer service and strong relationships are the keys to success. Take the time to get to know the people involved in your transaction, and you'll be on your way to achieving the best outcome for yourself and your family.

If you're looking for a referral to another agent in New Hampshire, Massachusetts, or anywhere in the country, I can help you. I have a vast network of agents who are excellent at taking really good care of their clients, and I'd be happy to match you with someone who is a great fit for you.

I hope you use this book as a resource when you're ready to sell your home, and you now feel well-equipped to partner with the right listing agent who can help you get the best deal for your home. If you're in the Lakes Region, I'd love the opportunity to meet with you. If you're looking for additional resources for buying or selling your home, visit CriticalDecisionsBooks.com/Resources. I regularly update these tools, guides, lists, and articles so you have access to the most up-to-date information.

If you have questions, want to discuss your real estate goals, need help with a referral, would like to share your thoughts about this book, or just want to connect, I love meeting new people. Please reach out! You can contact me at Michelle@PalysRealty.com. I will always find a way to make time for you or someone you refer to me.

And if you love boating on Lake Winnipesaukee, maybe we'll meet on the lake! I also love bringing buyers to view lake homes by boat so they can get the full experience.

Thank you for the time you've invested in reading this book. My goal is for you to use this information so you can sell quickly and profit well.

ABOUT THE AUTHOR

Michelle Palys, owner of eXp Realty at Village West in Gilford, NH, has been an entrepreneur since age 21. With two decades in real estate and thousands of transactions behind her, including 30 of her own— she has owned homes to condos, lakeside, seasonals, commercial spaces and fixer-uppers. Her hands-on experience gives her a sharp eye for potential and a deep understanding at every stage of the process.

Michelle served as her own general contractor on projects, designing layouts, managing vendors, and navigating approvals with local boards. She bought, grew and sold successful businesses including Allegory Inn, Along the River Campground, and the 302 Grill food truck in the White Mountains. With a background in mortgage lending, tax strategy, and hospitality, Michelle brings financial insight and creative thinking to every transaction. Add the ability to renovate and move around walls in her mind, possibilities are endless for her clients.

She's a certified high-performance coach and voice coach, known for clear communication and strategic guidance. Michelle won awards for her photography and photographed real estate from helicopters—long before drones were common.

She has taught photography and is always looking for new ways to market properties through photos and video.

Based in the Lakes Region, she relocated from Bedford, NH after her two children had grown. Michelle leads her Gilford office as a hub for connection and collaboration among professionals, trades people and local business owners around the lake.

Clients love Michelle for her efficient, well-informed style and exceptional customer service. They appreciate how detailed she is when it comes to protecting their financial position and real estate assets, negotiating strong for them and delivering great results with her smooth process.

In her free time, you'll find Michelle boating on Lake Winnipesaukee with family, friends, clients and her boat dog, Hannah or photographing properties. She enjoys live music, cards, games and traveling to places like Nashville and Italy. She's always looking to create more connections as she has for years, through masterminds around the globe. Find out for yourself. Connect with Michelle.

CONTACT

Michelle Palys
(*Palys* is pronounced *palace*, like a castle)

Website:	MichellePalys.com
Book Resources:	CriticalDecisionsBooks.com/Resources
Email:	Michelle@PalysRealty.com
LinkedIn:	MichellePalys
Facebook:	MichellePalysRealEstate